The Valley of S

Window⌣

Brinsley MacNamara

Alpha Editions

This edition published in 2024

ISBN : 9789362091314

Design and Setting By
Alpha Editions
www.alphaedis.com
Email - info@alphaedis.com

Contents

PREFATORY NOTE...- 1 -

CHAPTER I ....- 4 -

CHAPTER II...- 10 -

CHAPTER III ....- 14 -

CHAPTER IV ....- 21 -

CHAPTER V ....- 25 -

CHAPTER VI ....- 30 -

CHAPTER VII..- 37 -

CHAPTER VIII ....- 42 -

CHAPTER IX ....- 49 -

CHAPTER X ....- 54 -

CHAPTER XI ....- 59 -

CHAPTER XII..- 63 -

CHAPTER XIII ....- 67 -

CHAPTER XIV ....- 72 -

CHAPTER XV...- 75 -

CHAPTER XVI ....- 81 -

CHAPTER XVII..- 84 -

CHAPTER XVIII...- 90 -

CHAPTER XIX ....- 96 -

CHAPTER XX...- 103 -

CHAPTER XXI ....- 108 -

CHAPTER XXII..- 112 -

CHAPTER XXIII...- 119 -

CHAPTER XXIV ....- 125 -

CHAPTER XXV...- 128 -

CHAPTER XXVI ....- 133 -

CHAPTER XXVII ....- 138 -

CHAPTER XXVIII..- 144 -

CHAPTER XXIX ....- 153 -

CHAPTER XXX...- 158 -

CHAPTER XXXI ....- 169 -

CHAPTER XXXII ....- 173 -

PREFATORY NOTE

In the parlor, as they call it, or best room of every Irish farmhouse, one may come upon a certain number of books that are never read, laid there in lonely repose upon the big square table on the middle of the floor. A novel entitled "Knocknagow" is almost always certain to be amongst them, yet scarcely as the result of selection, although its constant occurrence cannot be considered purely accidental. There must lurk an explanation somewhere about these quiet Irish houses connecting the very atmosphere with "Knocknagow". A stranger, thinking of some of the great books of the world, would almost feel inclined to believe that this story of the quiet homesteads of Ireland must be one of them, a book full of inspiration and truth and beauty, a story sprung from the bleeding realities which were before the present comfort of these homes. Yet for all the expectations which might be raised up in one by this most popular, this typical Irish novel, it is most certainly the book with which the new Irish novelist would endeavor to contrast his own. For he would be writing of life, as the modern novelist's art is essentially a realistic one, and not of the queer, distant, half pleasing, half saddening thing which could make one Irish farmer's daughter say to another at any time within the past forty years:

"And you'd often see things happening nearly in real life like in 'Knocknagow.' Now wouldn't you?"

Nearer by a long way than Charles Joseph Kickham[Pg x] to what the Irish novelist should have been was William Carleton in his great, gloomy, melodramatic stories of the land. He was prevented by the agrarian obsession of his time from having the clear vision and wide pity, in keeping with his vehemence, which might have made him the Irish Balzac.

Even in Ireland Lever and Lover have become unpopular. They are read only by Englishmen who still try to perpetuate their comic convention when they write newspaper articles about Ireland.

As with Kickham, largely in his treatment of the Irish peasant, Gerald Griffin in "The Collegians" did not succeed in giving his Irish middle or "strong farmer" class characters the spiritual energy so necessary to the literary subject.

Here are five writers then, who included in their work such exact opposites as saints and sinners, heroes and *omadhanns*, earnest passionate men and *broths of bhoys*. And somehow between them, between those who wrote to degrade us and those who have idealized us, the real Irishman did not come to be set down. From its fiction, reality was absent, as from most other aspects of Irish life.

To a certain extent the realistic method has been employed by the dramatists of the Irish Literary Movement, but necessarily limited by the scope and conventions of the stage and by the narrower appeal of the spoken word in the mouth of an actor. The stage, too, has a way of developing cults and conventions and of its very nature must display a certain amount of artificiality, even in the handling of realistic material. Thus comes a sudden stagnation, a sudden completion always[Pg xi] of a literary movement developed mostly upon the dramatic side, as has come upon the work of the Abbey Theater.

It appears rather accidental, but perhaps on the whole to its benefit, that the dramatic form should have been adopted by J. M. Synge and not the epical form of the novel. Synge fell with a lash of surprise upon the Ireland of his time, for the Irish play had been as fully degraded as the Irish novel. Furthermore the shock of his genius created an opportunity which made possible the realistic Irish novelist. At the Abbey Theater they performed plays dealing with subjects which no Irish novelist, thinking of a public, would have dreamt of handling. Somehow their plays have come to be known and accepted throughout Ireland. Thus a reading public for this realistic Irish novel has been slowly created and the urge to write like this has come to many storytellers.

Of necessity, as part of the reaction from the work of the feeble masters we have known, the first examples of the new Irish novel were bound to be a little savage and pitiless. In former pictures of Irish life there was heavy labor always to give us the shade at the expense of the light, in fact at the expense of the truth which is life itself. In Ireland the protest of the realist is not so much against Romanticism as against an attempt made to place before us a pseudo-realism. According as the Irish people resign themselves to the fact that this is not a thing which should not be done, the work of the Irish realist will approximate more nearly to the quality of the Russian novelists, in which there are neither exaggerations of Light nor of Shade, but a picture of life all[Pg xii] gray and quiet, and brightened only by the beauty of tragic reality.

It leaves room for interesting speculation, that at a time of political chaos, at a time when in Ireland there is a great coming and going of politicians of all brands, dreamers, sages and mystics, the decline of the Irish Literary Movement on its dramatic side should have given the realistic Irish novelist his opportunity to appear. The urgent necessity of reality in Irish life at the moment fills one with the thought that a school of Irish realists might have brought finer things to the heart of Ireland than the Hy Brazil of the politicians.

The function of the Irish novelist to evoke reality has been proved in the case of "The Valley of the Squinting Windows." Upon its appearance the people of that part of Ireland with whom I deal in my writings became highly incensed. They burned my book after the best medieval fashion and resorted to acts of healthy violence. The romantic period seemed to have been cut out of their lives and they were full of life again. The story of my story became widely exaggerated through gradually increasing venom and my book, which had been well received by the official Irish Press,—whose reviewers generally read the books they write about—was supposed by some of my own people to contain the most frightful things. To the peasant mind, fed so long upon unreal tales of itself, the thing I had done became identified after the most incongruous fashion and very curiously with an aspect of the very literary association from which I had sprung. Language out of Synge's "Playboy of the Western World" came to my ears from every side during the days in which I was made to suffer for[Pg xiii] having written "The Valley of the Squinting Windows."

"And saving your presence, sir, are you the man that killed your father?"

"I am, God help me!"

"Well then, my thousand blessings to you!"

The country as a whole did not dislike my picture of Irish life or say it was untrue. It was only the particular section of life which was pictured that still asserted its right to the consolation of romantic treatment, but in its very attempt to retain romance in theory it became realistic in practise. It did exactly what it should have done a great many years ago with the kind of books from which it drew a certain poisonous comfort towards its own intellectual and political enslavement. The rest of Ireland was amused by the performance of those who did not think, with Mr. Yeats, that romantic Ireland was dead and gone. The realist had begun to evoke reality and no longer did a great screech sound through the land that this kind of thing should not be done. A change had come, by miraculous coincidence, upon the soul of Ireland. It was not afraid of realism now,—for it had faced the tragic reality of the travail which comes before a healthy national consciousness can be born. No longer would the realist be described in his own country as merely a morbid scoundrel or an enemy of the Irish people. They would not need again the solace of the sentimental novelist for all the offenses of the caricaturists in Irish fiction, because, with the wider and clearer vision of their own souls fully realized, had they already begun to look out upon the world.

BRINSLEY MACNAMARA.

Dublin, March 1st, 1919.

CHAPTER I

Mrs. Brennan took her seat again at the sewing-machine by the window. She sighed as she turned her tired eyes in search of some inducement to solace down the white road through the valley of Tullahanogue. The day was already bright above the fields and groups of children were beginning to pass through the morning on their way to school. Mrs. Brennan beheld their passage, yet now as always she seemed to miss the small beauty of the little pageant.

"God help them, the poor little things!" she condoled to herself, "and may He enlighten the unfortunate parents who send them to that quare, ould, ignorant pair, Master Donnellan and Mrs. Wyse, the mistress. Musha, sure they're no teachers!"

From this it might seem that Mrs. Brennan, the dressmaker of the valley and one well entitled to be giving out an opinion, did not think very highly of National Education. Yet it was not true that she failed to regard the lofty fact of education with all a peasant's stupid reverence, for was she not the mother of John Brennan, who was now preparing for the priesthood at a grand college in England? A priest, mind you! That was what you might call something for a woman to be!

The pride of her motherhood struck a high and resounding note in the life of the valley. Furthermore, it gave her authority to assert herself as a woman of remarkable standing amongst the people. She devoted her prerogative to the advancement of the Catholic Church. She manifested herself as one intensely interested in its welfare. There was no cheap religious periodical, from *The Catholic Times* to *The Messenger*, that she did not regularly purchase. All these she read to her husband, Ned Brennan, in the long quiet evenings after the manner of one discharging a religious duty.

This was a curious side of her. She kept him in comfort and in ease, and yet when his body had been contented she must needs apply herself to the welfare of his soul. For, although he spent many a penny of her money in the village of Garradrimna, was he not the father of John Brennan, who was going to be a priest of God? She forgave him everything on this account, even the coarse and blasphemous expressions he continually let fly from his mouth the while she read for him the most holy stories by Jesuit Fathers.

Just now she had given him two shillings with which to entertain himself. He had threatened to strike her in the event of her refusal.... That was why she had been sighing and why the tears were now creeping into her great tired eyes as she began to set her machine in motion for the tasks of the day. Dear,

dear, wasn't he the cruel, hard man?... Yet beyond all this thought of him was her bright dream of the day when, with the few pounds she had saved so secretly from the wide grasp of his thirst, she must fit him out in a rich suit of black and go by his side proudly to attend the ordination of their son John. It was because she so dearly loved her dream that she bore him with immense patience.

Also it was because she had been thinking of that grand day and of the descending splendor of her son that she now commented so strongly upon the passage of the children to school. She had spoken bitterly to her own heart, but in that heart of hers she was a bitter woman.

This was such a sunny, lovely morning. It was the day of the June Races in the town of Mullaghowen, and most of the valley-dwellers had gone there. The winding, dusty road through Tullahanogue was a long lane of silence amid the sunlight. It appeared as an avenue to the Palace of Dreams. So it was not at all strange that Mrs. Brennan was dreaming forward into the future and filling her mind with fancies of the past. She was remembering herself as Nan Byrne, the prettiest girl in the valley. This was no illusion of idle vanity, for was there not an old daguerreotype in an album on the table behind her at this very moment to prove that beauty had been hers? And she had been ruined because of that proud beauty. It was curious to think how her sister and she had both gone the same way.... The period of a generation had passed since the calamity had fallen upon them almost simultaneously. It was the greatest scandal that had ever happened in these parts. The holy priest, whose bones were now moldering beneath the sanctuary of the chapel, had said hard words of her. From the altar of God he had spoken his pity of her father, and said that she was a bad woman.

"May God strengthen him, for this is the bitter burden to bear. Philip Byrne is a decent man for all his daughter Nan is a woman of shame. I pray you avoid her every one who has the trace of God's purity in his heart. Let you go not into that house which she has made an abode of lust, nor allow the fair name of your own house to be blemished by the contamination of her presence within its walls."

Yes, it was true that all this had been said of her by the holy father, and in the very spot beneath which his bones were now at rest. They were the hard words surely to have issued from the lips of God's anointed. Even in the fugitive remembrance of them now they seemed to have left red marks like whip-lash weals across her soul. The burning hurt of them drove her deeper into remembrance. She had already come to the full development of her charms when her ambition had also appeared. It was, in short, to effect the "catch" of one of the strong farmers of the valley. She entered into conspiracy with her sister and, together, they laid their plans. Henry Shannon was the one upon whom she had set her eye and Loughlin Mulvey the one her sister Bridget had begun to desire. They were both men of family and substance, and hard drinkers after the fashion of the fields. They often called at the house to see the sisters. Philip Byrne, whose occupation as head-groom at the stables of the Moores of Garradrimna often took him away from Ireland, would always be absent during those visitations. But their mother would be there, Mrs. Abigail Byrne, ambitious for her daughters, in great style. It was never known to happen that either of the strong farmers called to the house without a bottle of whiskey. Mrs. Byrne always looked favorably upon them for their high decency, and the whiskey was good whiskey.

Here in this very room where she now sat remembering it all there had been such scenes! Her hair had been so thick and brown and there had been a rare bloom upon her skin as she had sat here alone with Henry Shannon, talking with him of queer things and kissing his dark, handsome face. And all through those far, bygone times she used to be thinking of his grand house and of his broad fields and the way she would one day assert herself in the joy of such possessions over her less fortunate sisters of the valley. Yet, ever mixed with her bright pieces of imagination, there had been such torturing doubts.... Her sister Bridget had always been so certain of her prey.

There had been times when Henry Shannon spent the night in the house. In those nights had been laid the foundations of her shame.... Very, very clearly did she remember the sickening, dreadful morning she had come to her mother with the story that she was going to have a child. How angry the elder woman had been, so lit within her all the wild instincts of the female against the betrayer of her sex? Why had she gone so far? Why had she not played her cards like her sister? There was no fear of her yet although she had got a proper hold of Loughlin Mulvey.... What was she to do at all? She who had had great ambitions was to become lower than the lowest in the valley.

Yet the three of them had conferred together, for all the others were so angry with her because of her disastrous condition into which she had allowed herself to slip without having first made certain of Henry Shannon. The only course left now was to "make a show" of him if he could not see his way to marry her.

She could now remember every line of the angry, misspelled letter she had sent to her whilom lover, and how it had brought him to the house in a mood of drunken repentance. He presented her with material for a new dress on the very same night, and, as she laughed and cried over it in turn, she thought how very curious it was that he should wish to see her figure richly adorned when already it had begun to put on those signs of disfigurement which announce the coming of a child. But he was very, very kind, and all suspicion fell away from her. Before he went he whispered an invitation to spend a few days with him in Dublin.... What did it matter now, and it was so kind of him to ask her? It showed what was in his mind, and therefore no talk of marriage passed between them. It did not seem necessary.

Then had followed quickly those lovely days in Dublin, she stopping with him as "Mrs. Henry Shannon" at a grand hotel. He had given her a wedding-ring, but while it remained upon her finger it was ever the little accusing symbol, filling her with an intense conviction of her sin.

This great adventure had marked the beginning of her acquaintance with the world beyond the valley, and, even now, through the gloom of her mood, she could remember it with a certain amount of gladness coming back to her mind. But it was queer that the brightest moment of her life should also have been the moment of darkest disaster.... She re-created the slight incidents of their quarrel. It was so strange of him after all the grand kindness he had just been showing her.... She had returned to the valley alone and with her disgrace already beginning to be heavy upon her.... She never saw Henry Shannon or spoke with him again. When she wrote referring distantly to their approaching marriage and making mention of the wedding-ring, the reply came back from Mr. Robinson, the solicitor in Garradrimna, who was his cousin and sporting companion. She knew how they had already begun to talk of her in the valley for having gone off to Dublin with Henry Shannon, and now, when an ugly word to describe her appeared there black and plain in the solicitor's letter, she felt, in blind shame, that the visit to Dublin had been planned to ruin her. The air of the valley seemed full of whispers to tell her that she had done a monstrous thing. Maybe they could give her jail for having done a thing like that, and she knew well that Henry Shannon's people would stop at nothing to destroy her, for they were a dark, spiteful crew. They were rich and powerful, with lawyers in the family, and what chance would she have in law now that every one was turned against her. So that night she went out when it was very dark and threw away the wedding-ring. The small, sad act appeared as the renunciation of her great ambition.

She remembered with a surpassing clearness the wide desolation of the time that followed. Loughlin Mulvey had been compelled to marry her sister Bridget because he had not been clever enough to effect a loophole of escape like Henry Shannon. Already three months after the marriage (bit by bit was she now living the past again) the child had been born to Bridget, and now she herself was waiting for the birth of her child.... Indeed Bridget need not have been so angry.

She had been delirious and upon the brink of death, and when, at last, she had recovered sufficiently to realize the sharpness of her mother's tongue once more the child had disappeared. She had escaped to England with all that was left of her beauty. There she had met Ned Brennan, and there had her son John Brennan been born. For a short while she had known happiness. Ned was rough, but in his very strength there was a sense of security and protection which made him bearable. And there was little John. He was not a bit like her short, wild impression of the other little child. Her disgrace had been the means of bringing Philip Byrne to his grave; and, after six or seven years, her mother had died, and she had returned to the valley of Tullahanogue. It was queer that, with all her early knowledge of the people of the valley, she had never thought it possible that some of them would one day impart to him the terrible secret she had concealed so well while acting the ingenuous maiden before his eyes.

Yet they were not settled a month at the cottage in the valley when Ned came from Garradrimna one night a changed man. Larry Cully, a loafer of the village, had attacked him with the whole story.... Was this the kind of people among whom she had brought him to live, and was this a fact about her? She confessed her share, but, illtreat her how he would, she could not tell him what had been done with the child.

Henceforth he was so different, settling gradually into his present condition. He could not go about making inquiries as to the past of his wife, and the people of the valley, gloating over his condition, took no pains to ease his mind. It was more interesting to see him torture himself with suspicion. They hardly fancied she had told him all. It was grand to see him drinking in his endeavors to forget the things he must needs be thinking of.

Thus had Mrs. Brennan lived with her husband for eighteen years, and no other child had been born to them. His original occupation of plumber's laborer found no opportunity for its exercise in the valley, but he sometimes lime-washed stables and mended roofs and gutters. For the most part, however, she kept him through her labor at the machine.

Her story was not without its turn of pathos, for it was strange to think of her reading the holy books to him in the long, quiet evenings all the while he despised her for what she had been with a hatred that all the magnanimous examples of religion could not remove.

She was thinking over it all now, and so keenly, for he had just threatened to strike her again. Eighteen years had not removed from his mind the full and bitter realization of her sin.... They were both beginning to grow gray, and her living atonement for what she had been, her son John who was going on for the Church, was in his twentieth year. Would her husband forgive her when he saw John in the garb of a priest? She wondered and wondered.

So deep was she in this thought that she did not notice the entrance of old Marse Prendergast, who lived in a cabin just across the road. Marse was a superannuated shuiler and a terror in the valley. The tears had been summoned to her eyes by the still unchanging quality of Ned's tone. They were at once detected by the old woman.

"Still crying, are ye, Nan Byrne, for Henry Shannon that's dead and gone?"

This was a sore cut, but it was because of its severity that it had been given. Marse Prendergast's method was to attack the person from whom she desired an alms instead of making an approach in fear and trembling.

"Well, what's the use in regretting now that he didn't marry ye after all?... Maybe you could give me a bit of Ned's tobacco for me little pipe, or a few coppers to buy some."

"I will in troth," she said, searching her apron pocket, only to discover that Ned had taken all her spare coppers. She communicated her regrets to the old woman, but her words fell upon ears that doubted.

"Ah-ha, the lie is on your lip yet, Nan Byrne, just as it was there for your poor husband the day he married you, God save us all from harm—you who were what you were before you went away to England. And now the cheek you have to go refuse me the few coppers. Ye think ye're a great one, don't you, with your son at college, and he going on to be a priest. Well, let me tell you that a priest he'll never be, your grand son, John. Ye have the quare nerve to imagine it indeed if you ever think of what happened to your other little son.... Maybe 'tis what ye don't remember that, Nan Bryne.... The poor little thing screeching in the night-time, and some one carrying a box out into the garden in the moonlight, and them digging the hole.... Ah, 'tis well I know all that, Nan Byrne, although you may think yourself very clever and mysterious. And 'tis maybe I'll see you swing for it yet with your refusals and the great annoyance you put me to for the means of a smoke, and I a real ould woman and all. But listen here to me, Nan Byrne! 'Tis maybe to your grand son, John Brennan, I'll be telling the whole story some day!"

CHAPTER II

Her tongue still clacking in soliloquy, Marse Prendergast hobbled out of the house, and Mrs. Brennan went to the small back window of the sewing-room. She gazed wistfully down the long, sloping fields towards the little lake which nestled in the bosom of the valley. Within the periods of acute consciousness which came between her sobs she began to examine the curious edifice of life which housed her soul. An unaccountable, swift power to do this came to her as she saw the place around which she had played as a child, long ago, when she had a brow snow-white and smooth, with nice hair and laughing eyes. Her soul, too, at that time was clean—clean like the water. And she was wont to have glad thoughts of the coming years when she had sprung to girlhood and could wear pretty frocks and bind up her hair. Across her mind had never fallen the faintest shadow of the thing that was to happen to her.

Yet now, as she ran over everything in her mind, she marveled not a little that, although she could not possibly have returned to the perfect innocence of her childhood state, she had triumphed over the blight of certain circumstances to an extraordinary extent. She was surprised to realize that there must have been some strength of character in her not possessed by the other women of the valley. It had been her mother's mark of distinction, but the dead woman had used it towards the achievement of different ends. Ends, too, which had left their mark upon the lives of both her daughters.

It struck her now, with another lash of surprise, that it had been an amazingly cheeky thing to have returned to the valley; but, as the shining waters of the lake led her mind into the quiet ways of contemplation, she could not help thinking that she had triumphed well.

To be living here at all with such a husband, and her son away in England preparing for the priesthood, seemed the very queerest, queerest thing. It was true that she held herself up well and had a fine conceit of herself, if you please. The mothers of the neighborhood had, for the most part, chosen to forget the contamination that might have arisen from sending their daughters to a woman like her for their dresses, and, in consequence, she had been enabled to build up this little business. She asserted herself in the ways of assertion which were open to the dwellers in the valley. She attended to her religious duties with admirable regularity. It was not alone that she fulfilled the obligation of hearing Mass on Sundays and Holydays, but also on many an ordinary morning when there was really no need to be so very pious. She went just to show them that she was passionately devoted to religion. Yet her neighbors never once regarded her in the light of a second Mary Magdalene. They entered into competition with her, it was true, for they could not let it be said that Nan Byrne was more religious than they, and so, between them, they succeeded in degrading the Mysteries. But it was the only way that was open to them of showing off their souls.

On a Sunday morning the procession they formed was like a flock of human crows. And the noise they made was a continual caw of calumny. The one presently absent was set down as the sinner. They were eternally the Pharisees and she the Publican. Mrs. Brennan was great among these crows of calumny. It was her place of power. She could give out an opinion coming home from Mass upon any person at all that would almost take the hearing out of your ears. She effectively beat down the voice of criticism against herself by her sweeping denunciations of all others. It was an unusual method, and resembled that of Marse Prendergast, the shuiler, from whom it may probably have been copied. It led many to form curious estimates as to the exact type of mind possessed by the woman who made use of it. There were some who described it as "thickness," a rather remarkable designation given to a certain quality of temper by the people of the valley. But there was no denying that it had won for her a cumulative series of results which had built up about her something definite and original and placed her resolutely in the life of the valley.

She would often say a thing like this, and it might be taken as a good example of her talk and as throwing a light as well upon the conversation of those with whom she walked home the road from the House of God. A young couple would have done the best thing by marrying at the right age, and these long-married women with the queer minds would be putting before them the very worst prospects. Mrs. Brennan would distinguish herself by saying a characteristic thing:

"Well, if there's quarreling between them, and musha! the same is sure to be, the names they'll call one another won't be very nice for the *pedigree* is not too *clean* on either side of the house."

No word of contradiction or comment would come from the others, for this was a morsel too choice to be disdained, seeing that it so perfectly expressed their own thoughts and the most intimate wishes of their hearts. It was when they got home, however, and, during the remaining portion of the Sunday, their happy carnival of destructive gossip, that they would think of asking themselves the question—"What right had Nan Byrne of all people to be thinking of little slips that had happened in the days gone by?" But the unreasonableness of her words never appeared in this light to her own mind. She was self-righteous to an enormous degree, and it was her particular fancy to consider all women as retaining strongly their primal degradation. And yet it was at such a time she remembered, not penitently however, or in terms of abasement, but with a heavy sadness numbing her every faculty. It was her connection with a great sin and her love for her son John which would not become reconciled.

When she returned to the valley with her husband and her young child she had inaugurated her life's dream. Her son John was to be her final justification before the world and, in a most wondrous way, had her dream begun to come true. She had reared him well, and he was so different from Ned Brennan. He was of a kindly disposition and, in the opinion of Master Donnellan, who was well hated by his mother, gave promise of great things. He had passed through the National School in some way that was known only to Mrs. Brennan, to "a grand College in England." He appeared as an extraordinary exception to the breed of the valley, especially when one considered the characters of both his parents.

Mrs. Brennan dearly loved her son, but even here, as in every phase of her life, the curious twist of her nature revealed itself. Hers was a selfish love, for it had mostly to do with the triumph he represented for her before the people of the valley. But this was her dream, and a dream may often become dearer than a child. It was her one sustaining joy, and she could not bear to think of any shadow falling down to darken its grandeur. The least suspicion of a calamity of this kind always had the effect of reducing to ruins the brazen front of the Mrs. Brennan who presented herself to the valley and of giving her a kind of fainting in her very heart.

Her lovely son! She wiped her tear-stained cheeks now with the corner of her black apron, for Farrell McGuinness, the postman, was at the door. He said, "Good-morra, Mrs. Brennan!" and handed her a letter. It was from John, telling her that his summer holidays were almost at hand. It seemed strange that, just now, when she had been thinking of him, this letter should have come.... Well, well, how quickly the time passed, now that the snow had settled upon her hair.

Farrell McGuinness was loitering by the door waiting to have a word with her when she had read her letter.

"I hear Mary Cooney over in Cruckenerega is home from Belfast again. Aye, and that she's shut herself up in a room and not one can see a sight of her. Isn't that quare now? Isn't it, Mrs. Brennan?"

"It's great, isn't it, Farrell? You may be sure there's something the matter with her."

"God bless us now, but wouldn't that be the hard blow to her father and mother and to her little sisters?"

"Arrah musha, between you and me and the wall, the divil a loss. What could she be, anyhow?"

"That's true for you, Mrs. Brennan!"

"Aye, and to think that it was in Belfast, of all places, that it happened. Now, d'ye know what I'm going to tell ye, Farrell? 'Tis the bad, Orange, immoral hole of a place is the same Belfast!"

CHAPTER III

Farrell McGuinness, grinning to himself, had moved away on his red bicycle, and a motor now came towards her in its envelope of dust down the long road of Tullahanogue. This was the first hire motor that had appeared in the village of Garradrimna and was the property of Charlie Clarke, an excellent, religious man, who had interested himself so successfully in bazaars and the charities that he had been thus enabled to purchase it. Its coming amongst them had been a sensational occurrence. If a neighbor wished to flout a neighbor it was done by hiring Clarke's car; and Mrs. Brennan immediately thought what a grand thing it would be to take it on the coming Thursday and make a brave show with her son John sitting up beside her and he dressed in black. The dignity of her son, now moving so near the priesthood, demanded such a demonstration. She hailed Charlie Clarke, and the car came suddenly to a standstill. The petrol fumes mingling with the rising dust of the summer road, floated to her nostrils like some incense of pride.

"Good morning, Mrs. Brennan!"

"Good morning, Mr. Clarke!"

"You're not at the races of Mullaghowen?"

"Not yet, Mrs. Brennan, but I'm going—and with the Houlihans of Clonabroney."

"The Houlihans of Clonabroney, well, well; that's what you might call a *quality* drive."

"Oh, indeed, 'tis almost exclusively to the quality and to the priests my drives are confined, Mrs. Brennan. I'm not patronized by the beggars of the valley."

"That's right, Mr. Clarke, that's right. Keep your car *clean* at all costs.... It's what I just stopped you to see if you could drive me over to Kilaconnaghan to meet my son John on Thursday. He's coming home."

"Is that so? Well you may say that's grand, Mrs. Brennan. Oh, indeed, John is the rare credit to you, so he is. You should be proud of him, for 'tis the fine beautiful thing to be going on for the Church. In fact, do ye know what it is, Mrs. Brennan? Only I'm married, I'd be thinking this very minute of giving up motor, shop, land and everything and going into a monastery. I would so."

"Now aren't you the fine, noble-minded man to be thinking of the like?"

"I am so.... Well, I'll drive you, Mrs. Brennan. On Thursday, you say, to Kilaconnaghan. The round trip will cost you fifteen shillings."

"Fifteen shillings?"

Charlie Clarke had already re-started the car which was again humming dustily down the road. Mrs. Brennan turned wearily into the sewing-room and seated herself once more by the machine. She was crushed a little by the thought of the fifteen shillings. She saw clearly before her the long procession of the hours of torture for her eyes that the amount represented. It appeared well that she had not given the few coppers to old Marse Prendergast, for, even as things stood, she must approach some of her customers towards the settlement of small accounts to enable her to spend fifteen shillings in the display of her pride.... For eighteen years it had been thus with her, this continual scraping and worrying about money. She wondered and wondered now was she ever destined to find release from mean tortures. Maybe when her son had become a priest he would be good to his mother? She had known of priests and the relatives of priests, who had grown amazingly rich.

She was recalled from her long reverie by the return of Ned Brennan from Garradrimna. The signs of drink were upon him.

"Where's me dinner?" he said, in a flat, heavy voice.

"Your dinner, is it? Oh dear, dear, 'tis how I never thought of putting it on yet. I had a letter from John, and sure it set me thinking. God knows I'll have it ready for you as soon as I can."

"Aye, John. A letter from John.... Begad.... Begad.... And I wanting me dinner!"

"So you'll have it, so you'll have it. Now aren't you the wild, impatient man? Can't you wait a minute?"

"I never did see such a woman as you, and I in a complete hurry. Three slates slipped down off the school roof in the bit of wind the other night, and I'm after getting instructions from Father O'Keeffe to put them on."

"Ah, sure, 'tis well I know how good and industrious you are, Ned. That's the sixth time this year you've put on the very same slates. You're a good man, indeed, and a fine tradesman."

For the moment his anger was appeased by this ironical compliment, which she did not intend as irony; but at heart he was deeply vexed because he was going to do this little job. She knew he must be talking of it for months to come. When the few shillings it brought him were spent she must give him others and others as a continuous reward for his vast effort. This she must do as a part of her tragic existence, while beholding at the same time how he despised her in his heart.

But, just now, the bitterness of this realization did not assail her with the full power of the outer darkness, for her mind was lit brilliantly to-day by the thought of John. And during the hours that passed after she had fitted out Ned for his adventurous expedition to the roof she could just barely summon up courage to turn the machine, so consumed was she by a great yearning for her son.

The days, until Thursday, seemed to stretch themselves into an age. But at three o'clock, when Charlie Clarke's white motor drew up at the door, she was still preparing for the journey. In the room which had known another aspect of her life she had been adorning herself for long hours. The very best clothes and all the personal ornaments in her possession must needs be brought into use. For it had suddenly appeared to her that she was about to enter into an unique ceremony comparable only to the ordination of John.

Searching in an unfrequented drawer of the dressing-table for hair-pins, she had come upon an old cameo-brooch, one of Henry Shannon's costly presents to her during the period of their strange "honeymoon." It was a pretty thing, so massive and so respectable-looking. It was of that heavy Victorian period to which her story also belonged. With trembling hands she fastened it upon her bosom. In a deeper recess of the drawer she came upon a powder puff in a small round box, which still held some of the aid to beauty remaining dry and useful through all the years. She had once used it to heighten her graces in the eyes of Henry Shannon. And now, for all the blanching trouble through which she had passed, she could not resist the impulses of the light woman in her and use it to assert her pride in her son. It must be a part of her decking-out as she passed through the valley in a motor for the first time, going forth to meet her son.

She took her seat at last by the side of Charlie Clarke, and passed proudly down the valley road. Things might have gone as agreeably as she had planned but for the peculiar religious warp there was in Charlie. He might have talked about the mechanism of his car or remarked at length upon the beauty of the summer day, but he must inevitably twist the conversation in the direction of religion.

"I suppose," said he, "that it's a fine thing to be the mother of a young fellow going on for the Church. It must make you very contented in yourself when you think of all the Masses he will say for you during your lifetime and all the Masses he will say for the repose of your soul when you are dead and gone."

"Aye, indeed, that's a grand and a true saying for you, Mr. Clarke. But sure what else could one expect from you, and yourself the good man that goes to Mass every day?"

"And, Mrs. Brennan, woman dear, to see him saying the Holy Mass, and he having his face shining with the Light of Heaven!"

"A beautiful sight, Mr. Clarke, as sure as you're there."

The car was speeding along merrily, and now it had just passed, with a slight bump, over the culvert of a stream, which here and there was playing musically about little stones, and here and there was like bits of molten silver spitting in the sun. It was a grand day.

Whether or not the unusual sensation of the throbbing car was too much for Mrs. Brennan, she was speaking little although listening eagerly to the words of Charlie Clarke, asking him once or twice to repeat some sentences she had been kept from hearing by the noise of the engine. Now she was growing more and more silent, for they had not yet passed out of the barony of Tullahanogue. She saw many a head suddenly fill many a squinting window, and men and women they met on the road turn round with a sneer to gaze back at her sitting up there beside Charlie Clarke, the saintly chauffeur who went to Mass every day.

Her ears were burning, and into her mind, in powerful battalions, were coming all the thoughts that had just been born in the minds of the others. The powder she had applied to her cheeks was now like a burning sweat upon her skin. The cameo-brooch felt like a great weight where it lay upon her bosom heavily. It caught her breath and so prevented her maintaining conversation with Charlie Clarke. It reminded her insistently of the dear baby head of John reposing, as in a bower of tenderness, upon the same place.

"It must be the grand and blessed thing for a mother to go to confession to her son. Now wouldn't it be wonderful to think of telling him, as the minister of God's mercy, the little faults she had committed before he was born or before she married his father. Now isn't that the queer thought, Mrs. Brennan?"

She did not reply, and it took all she could marshal of self-possession to protect her from tears as the motor hummed into the village of Kilaconnaghan, where the railway station was. They had arrived well in advance of the train's time. She passed through the little waiting-room and looked into the advertisement for Jameson's Whiskey, which was also a mirror. She remembered that it was in this very room she had waited before going away for that disastrous "honeymoon" with Henry Shannon.... This was a better mirror than the one at home, and she saw that the blaze upon her cheeks had already subdued the power of the powder, making it unnecessary and as the merest dirt upon her face.... The cameo-brooch looked so large and gaudy.... She momentarily considered herself not at all unlike some faded women of the pavement she had seen move, like malignant specters, beneath the lamplight in Dublin city.... She plucked away the brooch from her bosom and thrust it into her pocket. Then she wiped her face clean with her handkerchief.

Far off, and as a glad sound coming tentatively to her ears, she could hear the train that was bearing her beloved son home to the valley and to her. It was nearly a year since she last saw him, and she fancied he must have changed so within that space of time. Who knew how he might change towards her some day? This was her constant dread. And now as the increasing noise of the train told that it was drawing nearer she felt immensely lonely.

The few stray passengers who ever came to Kilaconnaghan by the afternoon train had got out, and John Brennan was amongst them. On the journey from Dublin he had occupied a carriage with Myles Shannon, who was the surviving brother of Henry Shannon and the magnate of the valley. The time had passed pleasantly enough, for Mr. Shannon was a well-read, interesting man. He had spoken in an illuminating way of the Great War. He viewed it in the light of a scourge and a just reckoning of calamity that the nations must pay for bad deeds they had done. "It is strange," said he, "that even a nation, just like an individual, must pay its just toll for its sins. It cannot escape, for the punishment is written down with the sin. There is not one of us who may not be made to feel the wide sweep of God's justice in this Great War, even you, my boy, who may think yourself far removed from such a possibility."

These were memorable words, and John Brennan allowed himself to fall into a spell of silence that he might the better ponder them. Looking up suddenly, he caught the other gazing intently at him with a harsh smile upon his face.

So now that they were to part they turned to shake hands.

"Good-by, Mr. Brennan!" said Myles Shannon to the student. "I wish you an enjoyable holiday-time. Maybe you could call over some evening to see my nephew Ulick, my brother Henry's son. He's here on holidays this year for the first time, and he finds the valley uncommonly dull after the delights of Dublin. He's a gay young spark, I can tell you, but students of physic are generally more inclined to be lively than students of divinity."

This he said with a flicker of his harsh smile as they shook hands, and John Brennan thanked him for his kind invitation. Catching sight of Mrs. Brennan, Mr. Shannon said, "Good-day!" coolly and moved out of the station.

To Mrs. Brennan this short conversation on the platform had seemed protracted to a dreadful length. As she beheld it from a little distance a kind of desolation had leaped up to destroy the lovely day. It compelled her to feel a kind of hurt that her son should have chosen to expend the few first seconds of his home-coming in talking, of all people, to one of the Shannon family. But he was a young gentleman and must, of course, show off his courtesy and nice manners. And he did not know.... But Myles Shannon knew.... His cool "Good-day!" to her as he moved out of the station appeared to her delicate sensitiveness of the moment as an exhibition of his knowledge. Immediately she felt that she must warn John against the Shannons.

He came towards her at last, a thin young man in black, wearing cheap spectacles. He looked tenderly upon the woman who had borne him. She embraced him and entered into a state of rapt admiration. Within the wonder of his presence she was as one translated, her sad thoughts began to fall from her one by one. On the platform of this dusty wayside station in Ireland she became a part of the glory of motherhood as she stood there looking with pride upon her son.

The motor had surprised him. He would have been better pleased if this expense had been avoided, for he was not without knowledge and appreciation of the condition of his parents' affairs. Besides the little donkey and trap had always appeared so welcome in their simplicity, and it was by means of them that all his former home-comings had been effected. Those easy voyages had afforded opportunity for contemplation upon the splendor of the fields, but now the fields seemed to slip past as if annoyed by their faithlessness. Yet he knew that his mother had done this thing to please him, and how could he find it in his heart to be displeased with her?

She was speaking kind words to him, which were being rudely destroyed, in their tender intonation, by the noise of the engine. She was setting forth the reasons why she had taken the car. It was the right thing now around Garradrimna.—The Houlihans of Clonabroney.—Again the changing of the gears cut short her explanation.

"That man who was down with you in the train, Mr. Shannon, what was he saying to you?"

"Indeed he was kindly inviting me over to see his nephew. I never knew he had a nephew, but it seems he has lived up in Dublin. He said that his brother, Henry Shannon, was the father of this young man."

The feelings which her son's words brought rushing into her mind seemed to cloud out all the brightness which, for her, had again returned to the day. Yes, this young man, this Ulick Shannon, was the son of Henry Shannon and Henry Shannon was the one who had brought the great darkness into her life.... It would be queer, she thought, beyond all the queerness of the world, to see the son of that man and her son walking together through the valley.

The things that must be said of them, the terrible sneer by which they would be surrounded—Henry Shannon's son and the son of Nan Byrne.... She grew so silent beneath the sorrow of her vision that, even in the less noisy spaces of the humming car, the amount of time during which she did not speak seemed a great while.

"What is the matter, mother?" said John Brennan.

"It was how I was thinking that maybe it would be better now if you had nothing to do with the Shannons."

"But it was very kind of Mr. Shannon to invite me."

"I know, I know; but I'd rather than the world it was any other family at all only the Shannons. They're a curious clan."

In the painful silence that had come upon them she too was thinking of the reasons from which her words had sprung. Of how Henry Shannon had failed to marry her after he had ruined her; of how the disgrace had done no harm at all to him with his money and his fine farm. Then there was the burning thought of how he had married Grace Gogarty, the proudest and grandest girl in the whole parish, and of how this young man had been born prematurely and, by a curious chance, about the same time as her own little child. The one thing that she always dreaded more than any other, in the pain of its remembrance, was the fact that Henry Shannon had married Grace Gogarty directly after the "honeymoon" with her in Dublin. Yes, it was hardest of all to think of that, and of how Grace Gogarty had so held up her head all through the short period of her wedded life with Henry Shannon. And after his death she had gone about with such conceited sorrowfulness in her widow's weeds.

These thoughts had passed through her mind with swift definition, each one cutting deeper the gap which separated her from the long-dreamt-of joy of John's home-coming. And her lovely son sitting up beside her had grown so silent.

As the car stopped by the house and Ned Brennan came out to meet them, unshaven and walking doggedly, she felt very certain that a shadow had settled down upon this particular return of John. The remembrance of her sin, from which it seemed impossible to escape, made the great thing she had planned so little and desolate.

CHAPTER IV

There arose a continual coming and going of John Brennan to and from the house of his mother through the valley. He was an object of curiosity and conjecture. The windows would squint at him as he went past through power of the leering faces behind; men working in the fields would run to the hedges and gaze after him as he went far down the road.

In the evenings black prophets would foregather and say: "Now isn't he the fine-looking young fellow indeed, with the grand black clothes upon him; but he'll never be a priest, and that's as sure as you're there, for his mother is Nan Byrne, and she was a bad woman, God help us all! 'Tis a pity of him, when you come to think of it, for it isn't his fault, happening as it did before he was born."

John Brennan was innocent of guile, and so he did not become aware of the attitude of those among whom he passed. He did not realize that in his own person he stood as an affront to them, that he was the Levite standing nearer God than they in their crude condition as clods of the earth. It was his mother who had created this position for him, for she had directed his studies towards divinity. If his natural abilities had won him the promise of any other elevation, it might not have annoyed them so deeply. But this was something they could not have been expected to bear, for not one amongst them had a son a priest, although they believed as implicitly as Mrs. Brennan in the virtue of religion, and there was always a feeling of intense righteousness upon them when they remembered her story.

Yet, although this was the way they looked upon him, they were not without a certain cringing respect for the realization he represented. Thus it was that when they spoke to him there was a touch of deference in their voices although there was a sneer in their hearts. It could not be expected that he should see them as they really were. Yet there were odd, great moments when his larger vision enabled him to behold them moving infinitesimally, in affright, beneath the shadow of the Divine Hand. He possessed a certain gift of observation, but it was superficial and of little consequence to his character for it flourished side by side with the large charity of his heart.

One morning he encountered old Marse Prendergast upon the road. She was gathering a few green sticks from the hedge-rows. She seemed to be always looking for the means of a fire, and, to John Brennan, there appeared something that touched him greatly in the spectacle of this whining old woman, from whom the spark of life was so quickly fading, having no comfort, even on a summer day, but just to be sitting over a few smoldering sticks, sucking at an old black pipe and breaking out into occasional converse with herself. She who had given birth to strong sons and lovely daughters sitting here in her little cabin alone. Her clutch was gone from her to America, to the streets, and to the grave.

John Brennan felt the pity of her, although he did not notice that the curtsey she gave him from the ditch was an essential portion of her contempt for the son of Nan Byrne (the cheek of him going on for to be a priest!), or that when she addressed him as *Mr.* Brennan it was in derision.

"And glory be to God, sure we'll soon have to be calling you *Father* Brennan!" she repeated, as if silently marveling at the impossibility of the combination of words.

He saw her move to accompany him down the road, her old back bent cruelly beneath the load of the weighty, green branches. He was touched, for he was not blind to the symbolism for which she stood, and offered to carry the branches for her, and she, accepting his offer, called down upon his head the blessing of God.

As they moved slowly along the road she recounted, in snatches between her questions regarding his life at college, all the intimate woes of her life. Her lamentations, as they drew near the cottage of Mrs. Brennan, attracted the attention of his mother, who saw a sight filling her eyes which cut her to the bone. She saw her son John, her hope and pride, conversing with Marse Prendergast, the long-tongued shuiler who tramped the country with her stories and in quest of more stories—Marse Prendergast who knew her secret as no other knew it, and who had so recently reminded her of that knowledge. And he was carrying her sticks along the public road in the full light of day.... So powerful was the hurt of her maternal feelings that she almost fainted sitting there by her machine.

When John came into the room she looked so pale that he fancied she must be ill. He inquired as to the causes of her condition, but she only replied that she would try to tell him when he had taken his breakfast.

As he was eating in silence she wondered what at all she could say to him or how she would attempt to place her view of things before him. This incident of the morning might be taken as a direct foreshadowing of what might happen if his foolish charity extended further down the valley. She did not dare to imagine what things he might be told or what stories might be suggested to his mind by the talk of the neighbors. But it was clearly her duty doubly to protect him from such a possibility. She saw that he had finished his breakfast.

"That was the quare thing you were doing just now, John? It was the quarest thing at all, so it was."

"Queer, mother; what was?"

"Talking to old Marse Prendergast, son, and she only a woman of the roads with a bad tongue on her."

"I only stopped talking with her, mother, so that I might carry her sticks. She was not able."

"And she used the fine opportunity, I'll warrant, to drag information out of you and carry it all through the valley. That's what she was at! That's what she was at!"

There was a kind of mournful wail in Mrs. Brennan's tones as if she saw in John's action of the morning some irretrievable distance placed between herself and him. The people of the valley loomed ever great as an army between her and the desire of her heart, and John had just now, as it were, afforded an opening to the enemy.

He received a certain amount of hurt from her words, for although he knew her only as his mother and a good woman who was well nigh faultless in her practise of the Christian religion, why was it that this simple action of his, with its slight touch of charity, was resented by her? Yet he allowed her to proceed without question, listening always with that high and fine attention which must have been the attitude of Christ as He listened to His Mother in Galilee.

She painted a picture of the valley for his consideration. She proceeded to do this with a great concern moving her, for she was quick to perceive the change in him since his last holidays. He was a man now, and it was to his manhood condition she appealed. She began to tell him, with such a rush of words, the life-histories of those around him. There was not a slight detail she did not go to great pains to enlarge, no skeleton she did not cause to jump from its cupboard and run alive once more through the valley. She painted a new portrait of every inhabitant in a way that amazed John, who had not known of such things.

But over his first feelings of surprise came a great realization of sadness. For this was his mother who was speaking. Hitherto he had looked upon her as one untouched by the clayey villainies of earth, a patient and very noble woman, with tired eyes and busy hands rather fashioned to confer benedictions than waste themselves in labor. Now he was listening to one most subtly different, to a woman who had been suddenly metamorphosed into the likeness of something primeval and startling. And she was oh! so bitter.

Mrs. Brennan had no notion of the change that had come upon her. To herself there still appeared no difference in herself. She was doing all this for love of her son John, as she had done much for love of him.

There fell a thick silence between them when she had finished. The mother and the son were both exhausted, he from listening to her and she from reading the pedigrees of every one to whom her mind could possibly extend, including Marse Prendergast, the shuiler, and the Shannons, who were almost gentlemen like the Houlihans of Clonabroney.

John Brennan sighed as he said out of the innocence of his heart:

"It is good, mother, that we are not as the rest of these."

Mrs. Brennan did not reply.

CHAPTER V

In rural Ireland the "bona-fide," or rather *mala-fide*, traveler constitutes a certain blasphemous aspect in the celebration of the Sabbath. There are different types of "bona-fide," whose characteristics may be said to vary in direct proportion to their love and enthusiasm for porter. The worship of porter, when it has attained the proportions of a perfect passion, is best described as "the pursuit of porter in a can." It is the cause of many drunken skirmishes with the law, and it is interesting to observe such mistaken heroes in the execution of their plans.

At a given signal a sudden descent is made upon a pub. A series of whistles from sentries in various parts of the village has announced the arrival of the propitious moment. A big tin'can is the only visible evidence of their dark intention. One almost forgets its betraying presence in the whirling moment of the brave deed. Then the deed is done. By some extraordinary process the can that was empty is found to be filled. It is the miracle of the porter.... When the sergeant and his colleagues come on the scene some hours later, an empty can with slight traces of froth upon the sides, "like beaded bubbles winking at the brim," constitutes the remaining flimsy evidence of the great thing that has happened.

The mind of John Brennan was more or less foreign to this aspect of life amongst the fields. He would be the very last to realize that such were essential happenings in the life of his native village of Garradrimna. On his first Sunday at home he went walking, after second Mass, through the green woods which were the western boundary of the village. His thoughts were dwelling upon Father O'Keeffe's material interpretation of the Gospel story. At last they eddied into rest as he moved there along the bright path between the tall trees, so quiet as with adoration.

When he came by that portion of the demesne wall, which lay at the back of Brannagan's public-house, he heard a scurrying of rabbits among the undergrowth. In the sudden hush which followed he heard a familiar voice raised in a tense whisper.

"Hurry, quick! quick! There's some one in black coming up the path. It must be Sergeant McGoldrick. The can! the can!"

His cheeks were suddenly flushed by a feeling of shame, for it was his father who had spoken. He stood behind a wide beech tree in mere confusion and not that he desired to see what was going forward.

His father, Ned Brennan, bent down like an acrobat across the demesne wall and took the can from some one beneath. Then he ran down through the undergrowth, the brown froth of the porter dashing out upon his trousers, his quick eyes darting hither and thither like those of a frightened animal. But he did not catch sight of John, who saw him raise the can to his lips.

It was a new experience for John Brennan to see his father thus spending the Sabbath in this dark place in the woods, while out in the young summer day spilled and surged all the wonder of the world.... A sort of pity claimed possession of him as he took a different way among the cathedral trees.... His father was the queer man, queer surely, and moving lonely in his life. He was not the intimate of his son nor of the woman who was his son's mother. He had never seemed greatly concerned to do things towards the respect and honor of that woman. And yet John Brennan could not forget that he was his father.

Just now another incident came to divert his mood. He encountered an ancient dryad flitting through the woods. This was Padna Padna, a famous character in Garradrimna. For all his name was that of the great apostle of his country, his affinities were pagan. Although he was eighty, he got drunk every day and never went to Mass. In his early days he had been the proprietor of a little place and the owner of a hackney car. When the posting business fell into decline, he had had to sell the little place and the horse and car, and the purchase money had been left for his support with a distant relative in the village. He was a striking figure as he moved abroad in the disguise of a cleric not altogether devoted to the service of God. He always dressed in solemn black, and his coat was longer than that of a civilian. His great hat gave him a downcast look, as of one who has peered into the Mysteries. His face was wasted and small, and this, with his partially blinded eyes behind the sixpenny spectacles, gave him a certain asceticism of look. Yet it was the way he carried himself rather than his general aspect which created this impression of him. He was very small, and shrinking daily. His eyes were always dwelling upon his little boots in meditation. Were you unaware of his real, character, you might foolishly imagine that he was thinking of high, immortal things, but he was in reality thinking of drink.

This was his daily program. He got up early and, on most mornings, crossed the street to Bartle Donohoe, the village barber, for a shave. Bartle would be waiting for him, his dark eye hanging critically as he tested the razor edge against the skin of his thumb. The little blade would be glinting in the sunlight.... Sometimes Bartle would become possessed of the thought that the morning might come when, after an unusually hard carouse on the previous night, he would not be responsible for all his razor might do, that it might suddenly leap out of his shivering hand and make a shocking end of Padna Padna and all his tyranny.... But his reputation as the drunkard with the steadiest hand in Garradrimna had to be maintained. If he did not shave Padna Padna the fact would be published in every house.

"Bartle Donohoe was too shaky to shave me this morning; too shaky, I say. Ah, he's going wrong, going wrong! And will ye tell me this now? How is it that if ye buy a clock, a little ordinary clock for a couple of shillings, and give it an odd wind, it'll go right; but a man, a great, clever man'll go wrong no matter what way ye strive for to manage him?"

If Bartle shaved him, Padna Padna would take his barber over to Tommy Williams's to give him a drink, which was the only payment he ever expected. After this, his first one, Padna Padna would say, "Not going to drink any more to-day," to which Bartle Donohoe would reply sententiously: "D'ye tell me so? Well, well! Is that a fact?"

Then, directly, he would proceed to take a little walk before his breakfast, calling at every house of entertainment and referring distantly to the fact that Bartle Donohoe had a shake in his hand this morning. "A shame for him, and he an only son and all!"

And thus did he spend the days of his latter end, pacing the sidewalks of Garradrimna, entering blindly into pubs and discussing the habits of every one save himself.

He was great in the field of reminiscence.

"Be the Holy Farmer!" he would say, "but there's no drinking nowadays tost what used to be longo. There's no decent fellows, and that's a fact. Ah, they were the decent fellows longo. You couldn't go driving them a place but they'd all come home mad. And sure I often didn't know where I'd be driving them, I'd be that bloody drunk. Aye, decent fellows! Sure they're all dead now through the power and the passion of drink."

So this was the one whom John Brennan now encountered amid the green beauty of the woodland places. To him Padna Padna was one of the immortals. Succeeding holiday after succeeding holiday had he met the ancient man, fading surely but never wholly declining or disappearing. The impulse which had prompted him to speak to Marse Prendergast a few days previously now made him say: "How are you, old man?" to Padna Padna.

The venerable drunkard, by way of immediate reply, tapped upon his lips with his fingers and then blew upon his fingers and whistled in cogitation. It was with his ears that he saw, and he possessed an amazing faculty for distinguishing between the different voices of different people.

"John Brennan!" he at length exclaimed, in his high, thin voice. "Is that John Brennan?"

"It is, the very one."

"And how are ye, John?"

"Very well, indeed, Padna. How are you?"

"Poorly only. Ah, John, this is the hard day on me always, the Sunday. I declare to me God I detest Sunday. Here am I marching through the woods since seven and I having no drink whatever. That cursed Sergeant McGoldrick! May he have a tongue upon him some day the color of an ould brick and he in the seventh cavern of Hell! Did ye see Ned?"

The sudden and tense question was not immediately intelligible to John Brennan. There were so many of the name about Garradrimna. Padna Padna pranced impatiently as he waited for an answer.

"Ah, is it letting on you are that you don't know who I mean, and you with your grand ecclesiastical learning and all to that. 'Tis your own father, Ned Brennan, that I mean. I was in a 'join' with him to get a can out of Brannigan's. Mebbe you didn't see him anywhere down through the wood, for I have an idea that he's going to swindle me. Did ye see him, I'm asking you?"

Even still John did not reply, for something seemed to have caught him by the throat and was robbing him of the power of speech. The valley, with its vast malevolence of which his mother had so recently warned him, was now driving him to say something which was not true.

"No, Padna, I did not see him!" he at last managed to jerk out.

"Mebbe he didn't manage to get me drink for me yet, and mebbe he did get it and is after drinking it somewhere in the shadows of the trees where he couldn't be seen. But what am I saying at all? Sure if he was drinking it there before me, where you're standing, I couldn't see him, me eyes is that bad. Isn't it the poor and the hard case to be blinded to such an extent?"

John Brennan felt no pity, so horrible was the expression that now struggled into those dimming eyes. He thought of a puzzling fact of his parentage. Why was it that his mother had never been able to save his father from the ways of degradation into which he had fallen, the low companions, the destruction of the valley; from all of which to even the smallest extent she was now so anxious to save her son?

Padna Padna was still blowing upon his fingers and regretting:

"Now isn't it the poor and the hard case that there's no decent fellows left in the world at all. To think that I can meet never a one now, me that spent so much of me life driving decent fellows, driving, driving. John, do ye know what it is now? You're after putting me in mind of Henry Shannon. He was the decentest fellow! Many's the time I drove him down to your grandmother's place when he wouldn't have a foot under him to leave

Garradrimna. That was when your mother was a young girl, John. Hee, hee, hee!"

John could not divine the reasons for the old man's glee, nor did he perceive that the mind of Padna Padna, even in the darkening stages of its end, was being lit by a horrible sneer at him and the very fact of his existence. Instead he grew to feel rather a stir of compassion for this old man, with his shattered conception of happiness such as it was, burning his mind with memories while he rode down so queerly to the grave.

As he moved away through the long, peaceful aisles of the trees, his soul was filled with gray questioning because of what he had just seen of his father and because of the distant connection of his mother with the incident. Why was it at all that his mother had never been able to save his father?

As he emerged from the last circle of the woods there seemed to be a shadow falling low over the fields. He went with no eagerness towards the house of his mother. This was Sunday, and it was her custom to spend a large portion of the Sabbath in speaking of her neighbors. But she would never say anything about his father, even though Ned Brennan would not be in the house.

CHAPTER VI

Just now there happened something of such unusual importance in the valley that Mrs. Brennan became excited about it. The assistant teacher of Tullahanogue Girls' School, Miss Mary Jane O'Donovan, had left, and a new assistant was coming in her stead. Miss O'Donovan had always given the making of her things to Mrs. Brennan, so she spoke of her, now that she was gone, as having been "a *very* nice girl." Just yet, of course, she was not in a position to say as much about the girl who was coming. But the entry of a new person into the life of the valley was a great event! Such new things could be said!

On Monday morning Mrs. Brennan called her son into the sewing-room to describe the imminent nature of the event. The sense of depression that had come upon him during the previous day did not become averted as he listened.

What an extraordinary mixture this woman who was his mother now appeared before his eyes! And yet he could not question her in any action or in any speech; she was his mother, and so everything that fell from her must be taken in a mood of noble and respectful acceptance. But she was without charity, and as he saw her in this guise he was compelled to think of his father and the incident of yesterday, and he could not help wondering. He suddenly realized that what was happening presently in this room was happening in every house down the valley. Even before her coming she was being condemned. It was beneath the shadow of this already created cloud she would have to live and move and earn her little living in the schoolhouse of Tullahanogue. John Brennan began to have some pity for the girl.

Ned Brennan now appeared at the door leading to the kitchen and beckoned to his wife. She went at his calling, and John noticed that at her return some part of her had fallen away. His father went from the house whistling at a pitch that was touched with delight.

"Where is my father bound for?"

"He's gone to Garradrimna, John, to order lead for the roof of the school. The valley behind the chimney is leaking again and he has to cobble it. 'Tis the great bother he gets with that roof, whatever sort it is. Isn't it a wonder now that Father O'Keeffe wouldn't put a new one on it, and all the money he gets so handy ...?"

"My father seems to be always at that roof. He used to be at it when I was going to school there."

The words of her son came to Mrs. Brennan's ears with a sound of sad complaint. It caused her to glimpse momentarily all the villainy of Ned

Brennan towards her through all the years, and of how she had borne it for the sake of John. And here was John before her now becoming reverently magnified in that part of her mind which was a melting tenderness. It was him she must now save from the valley which had ruined her man. Thus was she fearful again and the heart within her caused to become troubled and to rush to and fro in her breast like rushing water. Then, as if her whole will was sped by some fearful ecstasy, she went on to talk in her accustomed way of every one around her, including the stranger who had not yet come to the valley.

It was on the evening of this day that Rebecca Kerr, the new assistant teacher, came through the village of Garradrimna to the valley of Tullahanogue. Paddy McCann drove McDermott's hackney car down past the old castle of the De Lacys. It carried her as passenger from Mullaghowen, with her battered trunk strapped over the well. The group of spitting idlers crowding around Brannagan's loudly asserted so much as Paddy McCann and his cargo loomed out of the shadows beneath the old castle and swung into the amazing realities of the village. It was just past ten o'clock and the mean place now lay amid the enclosing twilight. The conjunctive thirsts for drink and gossip which come at this hour had attacked the ejected topers, and their tongues began to water about the morsel now placed before them.

A new schoolmistress, well, well! Didn't they change them shocking often in Tullahanogue? And quare-looking things they were too, every one of them. And here was another one, not much to look at either. They said this as she came past. And what was her name? "Kerr is her name!" said some one who had heard it from the very lips of Father O'Keeffe himself.

"Rebecca Kerr is her name," affirmed Farrell McGuinness, who had just left a letter for her at the Presbytery.

"Rebecca what? Kerr—Kerr—Kerr, is it?" sputtered Padna Padna; "what for wouldn't it be *Carr* now, just common and simple? But of course *Kerr* has a ring of the quality about it. *Kerr*, be God!"

These were the oracles of Garradrimna who were now speaking of her thus. But she had no thought of them at all as she glanced hurriedly at the shops and puzzled her brains to guess where the best draper's shop might be. She had a vague, wondering notion as to where she might get all those little things so necessary for a girl. She had a fleeting glimpse of herself standing outside one of those worn counters she was very certain existed somewhere in the village, talking ever so much talk with the faded girl who dispensed the vanities of other days, or else exchanging mild confidences with the vulgar and ample mistress of the shop, who was sure to be always floating about the place immensely. Yes, just there was the very shop with its brave selection from the fashions of yester-year in the fly-blown windows.

And there was the Post Office through which her letters to link her with the outer world would come and go. She quickly figured the old bespectacled postmistress, already blinded partially, and bent from constant, anxious scrutiny, poring exultantly over the first letters that might be sent to "Miss Rebecca Kerr," and examining the postmark. Then the quality and gender of the writing, and being finally troubled exceedingly as to the person it could have come from—sister, mother, brother, father, friend, or "boy." Even although the tall candles of Romance had long since guttered and gone out amid the ashes of her mind the assaulting suspicion that it was from "a boy" would drive her to turn the letter in her hand and take a look at the flap. Then the temptation that was a part of her life would prove too strong for her and a look of longing would come into the dull eyes as she went hobbling into the kitchen to place it over the boiling kettle and so embark it upon its steamy voyage to discovery. In a few minutes she would be reading it, her hands trembling as she chuckled in her obscene glee at all the noble sentiments it might contain. The subsequent return of the letter to the envelope after the addition of some gum from a penny bottle if the old sticking did not suffice. Her interludiary sigh of satisfaction when she remembered that one could re-stick so many opened envelopes with a penny bottle of gum by using it economically. The inevitable result of this examination, a superior look of wisdom upon the withered face when the new schoolmistress, Rebecca Kerr, came for the first time into the office to ask for a letter from her love.... But so far in her life she had formed no deep attachment.

It was thus and thus that Rebecca Kerr ran through her mind a few immediate sketchy realizations of this village in Ireland. She had lived in others, and this one could not be so very different.... There now was the butcher's stall, kept filthily, where she might buy her bit of beef or mutton occasionally. She caught a glimpse of the victualler standing with his dirty wife amid the strong-smelling meat. The name above the door was that of the publichouse immediately beside it. A little further on, upon the same side, was the newsagent's and stationer's, where they sold sweets and everything. It was here she might buy her notepaper to write to her own people in Donegal, or else to some of her college friends with whom she still kept up a correspondence. And here also she might treat herself, on rare occasions, to a box of cheap chocolates, or to some of the injurious, colored sweets which always gave her the toothache, presenting the most of them, perhaps, to some child to whom she had taken a fancy.

By little bits like these, which formed a series of flashes, she saw some aspects of the life she might lead here. Each separate flash left something of an impression before it went out of her mind.

The jingling car swung on past the various groups upon the street, each group twisting its head as one man to observe the spectacle of her passing. "That's the new schoolmistress!" "There she is, begad!" "I heard Paddy McCann saying she was coming this evening!" She was now in line with the famous house of Tommy Williams, the gombeen-man. She knew from the look of it that it was here she must buy her few groceries, for this was the principal house in Garradrimna and, even so far as she, the octopus of Gombeenism was sure to extend itself. To be sure, the gombeen-man would be the father of a family, for it is the clear duty of such pillars of the community to rear up a long string of patriots. If those children happened to be of school-going age, it was certain they would not be sent to even the most convenient school unless the teachers dealt in the shop. This is how gombeenism is made to exercise control over National Education. Anyhow Rebecca Kerr was very certain that she must enter the various-smelling shop to discuss the children with the gombeen-man's wife.

It was indeed a dreary kind of life that she would be compelled to lead in this place, and, as she passed the pretty chapel, which seemed to stand up in the sight of Heaven as excuse for the affront that was Garradrimna, she had a strange notion how she must go there sometimes to find respite from the relentless crush of it all. On bitter evenings, when her mind should ring with the mean tumults of the life around her, it was there only she might go and, slipping in through the dim vestibule where there were many mortuary cards to remind her of all the dead, she would walk quickly to the last pew and, bending her throbbing head, pour out her soul in prayer with the aid of her little mother-of-pearl rosary.... They had gone a short distance past the chapel and along the white road towards the valley.

"This is the place," said Paddy McCann.

She got down from the car wearily, and McCann carried her battered trunk into the house of Sergeant McGoldrick which had been assigned as her lodging by Father O'Keeffe. He emerged with a leer of expectation upon his countenance, and she gave him a shilling from her little possessions. At the door she was compelled to introduce herself.

"So you are the new teacher. Well, begad! The missus is up in the village. Come in. Begad!"

He stood there, a big, ungainly man, at his own door as he gave the invitation, a squalling baby in his arms, and in went Rebecca Kerr, into the sitting-room where Mrs. McGoldrick made clothes for the children. The sergeant proceeded to do his best to be entertaining. She knew the tribe. He remained smoking his great black pipe and punctuated the squalls of the baby by spitting huge volumes of saliva which hit the fender with dull thuds.

"It's a grand evening in the country," said Sergeant McGoldrick.

"Yes, a nice evening surely," said Rebecca Kerr.

"Oh, it was a grand, lovely day in the country, the day. I was out in the country all through the day. I was collecting the census of the crops, so I was; a difficult and a critical job, I can tell you!"

With an air of pride he took down the books of lists and showed her the columns of names and particulars.... It was stupidly simple. Yet here was this hulk of a man expanding his chest because of his childish achievement. He had even stopped smoking and spitting to give space to his own amazement, and the baby had ceased mewling to marvel in infantile wonder at the spacious cleverness of her da.

After nearly half an hour of this performance Mrs. McGoldrick bustled into the room. She was a coarse-looking woman, whose manner had evidently been made even more harsh by the severe segregation to which the wives of policemen are subjected. Her voice was loud and unmusical, and it appeared to Rebecca from the very first that not even the appalling cleverness of her husband was a barrier to her strong government of her own house. The sergeant disappeared immediately, taking the baby with him, and left the women to their own company. Mrs. McGoldrick had seen the battered, many-corded trunk in the hall-way, and she now made a remark which was, perhaps, natural enough for a woman:

"You haven't much luggage anyway!" was what she said.

"No!" replied Rebecca dully.

Then she allowed her head to droop for what seemed a long while, during all of which she was acutely conscious that the woman by her side was staring at her, forming impressions of her, summing her up.

"I don't think you're as tall as Miss O'Donovan was, and you haven't as nice hair!"

Rebecca made no comment of any kind upon this candor, but now that the way had been opened Mrs. McGoldrick poured out a flood of information regarding the late assistant of the valley school. She was reduced to little pieces and, as it were, cremated in the furnace of this woman's mind until tiny specks of the ashes of her floated about and danced and scintillated before the tired eyes of Rebecca Kerr.

As the heavier dusk of the short, warm night began to creep into the little room her soul sank slowly lower. She was hungry now and lonely. In the mildest way she distantly suggested a cup of tea, but Mrs. McGoldrick at once resented this uncalled-for disturbance of her harangue by bringing out what was probably meant to be taken as the one admirable point in the other girl's character.

"Miss O'Donovan used always get her own tea."

But the desolating silence of Rebecca at length drove her towards the kitchen, and she returned, after what seemed an endless period, with some greasy-looking bread, a cup without a handle, and a teapot from which the tea dribbled in agony on to the tablecloth through a wound in its side.

The sickening taste of the stuff that came out of the teapot only added to Rebecca's sinking feeling. Her thoughts crept ever downward.... At last there came a blessed desire for sleep-sleep and forgetfulness of this day and the morrow. Her head was already beginning to spin as she inquired for her room.

"Your room?" exclaimed Mrs. McGoldrick in harsh surprise. "Why, 'tis upstairs. There's only two rooms there, myself and the sergeant's and the lodger's room—that's yours. I hadn't time this week back to make the bed since Miss O'Donovan left, but of course you'll do that for yourself. The sergeant is gone up to the barracks, so I'll have to help you carry up your box, as I suppose you'll be wanting to get out some of your things."

It was a cruelly hard job getting the trunk up the steep staircase, but between them they managed it. Rebecca was not disappointed by the bare, ugly room. Mrs. McGoldrick closed the door behind them and stood in an attitude of expectation. Even in the present dull state of her mind Rebecca saw that her landlady was, with tense curiosity, awaiting the opening of the box which held her poor belongings.... Then something of the combative, selfish attitude of the woman to her kind stirred within her, and she bravely resolved to fight, for a short space, this prying woman who was trying to torment her soul.

She looked at the untidied bed with the well-used sheets.... What matter? It was only the place whereon the body of another poor tortured creature like herself had lain. She would bear with this outrage against her natural delicacy.

In perfect silence she took off her skirt and blouse and corset. She let fall her long, heavy hair and, before the broken looking-glass, began to dally wearily with its luxuriance. This hair was very fair and priceless, and it was hers who had not great possessions. Her shining neck and blossomy breasts showed as a pattern in ivory against the background that it made.... Some man, she thought, would like to see her now and love her maybe. Beyond this vision of herself she could see the ugly, anxious face of the woman behind her. She could feel the discord of that woman's thoughts with the wandering strands of withering hair.

No word had passed between them since they came together into the room, and Mrs. McGoldrick, retreating from the situation which had been created, left with abruptness, closing the door loudly behind her.

With as much haste as she could summon, Rebecca took off her shoes and got her night-gown out of the trunk. Then she threw herself into the bed. She put out the light and fumbled in her faded vanity bag for her little mother-of-pearl rosary. There was a strange excitement upon her, even in the final moments of her escape, and soon a portion of her pillow was wet with tears. Between loud sobs arose the sound of her prayers ascending:

"Hail, Mary, full of grace, the Lord is with thee; blessed art thou amongst women, and blessed is the fruit of thy womb, Jesus.... Hail, Mary, full of grace, the Lord is with thee; blessed art thou.... Hail, Mary, full of grace...."

CHAPTER VII

At tea-time Mrs. Brennan was still talking to John of the girl who was coming to the valley. Outside the day was still full of the calm glory of summer. He went to the window and looked down upon the clean, blue stretch of the little lake.... He had grown weary of his mother's talk. What possible interest could he have in this unknown girl? He took a book from a parcel on the table. With this volume in his hand and reading it, as he might his breviary at some future time, he went out and down towards the lake. On his way, he met a few men moving to and from their tasks in the fields. He bade them the time of day and spoke about the beauty of the afternoon. As they replied, a curious kind of smile played around their lips, and there was not one who failed to notice his enviable condition of idleness.

"Indeed 'tis you that has the fine times!" "Indeed you might say 'tis you that has the fine times!" "Now isn't the learning the grand thing, to say that when you have it in your head you need never do a turn with your hands?"

Their petty comments had the effect of filling him with a distracting sense of irritation, and it was some time before he could pick up any continued interest in the book. It was the story of a young priest, such as he might expect to be in a few years. Suddenly it appeared remarkable that he should be reading this foreshadowing of his future. That he should be seeing himself with all his ideas translated into reality and his training changed into the work for which he had been trained. Strange that this thought should have come into his mind with smashing force here now and at this very time. Hitherto his future had appeared as a thing apart from him, but now it seemed intimately bound up with everything he could possibly do.

He began to see very clearly for the first time the reason for his mother's anxiety to keep him apart from the life of the valley. Did it spring directly from her love for him, or was it merely selfish and contributory to her pride? The whole burden of her talk showed clearly that she was a proud woman. He could never come to have her way of looking at things, and so he now felt that if he became a priest it was she and not himself who would have triumphed.... He was still reading the book, but it was in a confused way and with little attention. The threads of the story had become entangled somehow with the threads of his own story.... Occasionally his own personality would cease to dominate it, and the lonely woman in the cottage, his mother sitting in silence at her machine, would become the principal character.... The hours went past him as he pondered.

The evening shadows had begun to steal down from the hills. The western sky was like the color of a golden chalice. Men were coming home weary from the labor of the fields; cows were moving towards field gates with wise looks in their eyes to await the milking; the young calves were lowing for their evening meal. The quiet fir trees, which had slept all through the day, now seemed to think of some forgotten trust and were like vigilant sentries all down through the valley of Tullahanogue.

Suddenly the eyes of John Brennan were held by a splendid picture. The sweep of the Hill of Annus lay outlined in all the wonder of its curve, and, on the ridge of it, moving with humped body, was Shamesy Golliher, the most famous drunkard of the valley. He passed like a figure of destruction above the valley against the sunset. John smiled, for he remembered him and his habits, as both were known far and wide. He was now going towards a certain wood where the rabbits were plentiful. His snares were set there. The thin, pitiful cry of the entrapped creature now split the stillness, and the man upon the sweep of the world began to move with a more determined stride.... John Brennan, his mind quickening towards remembrance of incidents of his boyhood, knew that the cunning of Shamesy Golliher had triumphed over the cunning of the rabbits. Their hot little eager bodies must soon be sold for eightpence apiece and the money spent on porter in Garradrimna. It was strange to think of this being the ultimate fate of the rabbits that had once frisked so innocently over the green spaces of the woods.... He listened, with a slight turn of regret stirring him, until the last squeal had been absorbed by the stillness. Then he arose and prepared to move away from the lake. He was being filled by a deadly feeling of sadness. Hitherto the continuous adventure of adolescence had sustained him, but now he was a man and thinking of his future.

On his way across the sweep of the hill he encountered Shamesy Golliher. The famous drunkard was laden with the rabbits he had just taken from the snares. The strength of his thirst had also begun to attack him, so that by reason of both defects his legs now bent under him weakly as he walked. Yet his attitude did not suggest defeat, for he had never failed to maintain his reputation in the valley. He was the local bard, the satiric poet of the neighborhood. He was the only inhabitant of the valley who continually did what he pleased, for he throve within the traditional Gaelic dread of satire. No matter how he debased himself no man or woman dared talk of it for fear they might be made the subject of a song to be ranted in the taprooms of Garradrimna. And he was not one to respect the feelings of those whom he put into his rimes, for all of them were conceived in a mood of ribald and malignant glee.

"Me sound man John, how are ye?" he said, extending a white, nervous hand.

"I'm very well, thanks; and how are you, Shamesy?"

"Ah, just only middling. I don't look the very best. You'll excuse me not being shaved. But that's on account of the neuralgia. God blast it! it has me near killed. It has the nerves destroyed on me. Look at me hand." ... It was the idiosyncrasy of Shamesy Golliher to assert that drink was no part of his life.

Immediately he dropped into his accustomed vein. He gazed down the Hill of Annus and found material for his tongue. There were the daughters of Hughie Murtagh. They had no brother, and were helping their father in the fields.

"Them's the men, them's the men!" said Shamesy, "though glory be to God! 'twill be the hard case with them when they come to be married, for sure you wouldn't like to marry a man, now would you? And for pity's sake will you look at Oweneen Kiernan, the glutton! I hear he ate five loaves at the ball in Ballinamult; and as sure as you're there that powerful repast'll have to be made the material for a song."

A loud laugh sprang from the lips of Shamesy Golliher and floated far across the lake, and John Brennan was immediately surprised to find himself laughing in the same way.

The rimer was still pursuing Oweneen down the field of his mind.

"Aye, and I thank ye, ye'll see him doing his best after the new schoolmistress that's coming to us this evening. There's a great look-out, I can tell you, to see what kind she'll be. Indeed the last one wasn't much. Grand-looking whipsters, moryah! to be teaching the young idea. Indeed I wouldn't be at all surprised to see one of them going away from here sometime and she in the family way, although may God pardon me for alluding to the like and I standing in the presence of the makings of a priest!"

John Brennan felt himself blushing ever so slightly.

"And who d'ye think was in Garradrimna this evening? Why Ulick Shannon, and he a big man. Down to stop with his uncle Myles he is for a holiday. He wasn't here since he was a weeshy gosoon; for, what d'ye think, didn't his mother and father send him away to Dublin to be nursed soon after he was born and never seemed to care much about him afterwards; but they were the quare pair, and it was no good end that happened to themselves, for Henry Shannon and the girl he married, Grace Gogarty, both died within the one year. He in the full pride of his red life, and she while she was gallivanting about the country wearing mourning for him and looking for another husband that she never got before she went into the clay. Well, to make a long story short, Myles Shannon looked after the orphan, paying for his rearing and his education, and having him live as a gentleman in Dublin—

until now he's a great-looking fellow entirely, and going on, I suppose, for Doctoring, or the Law, or some other profitable devilment like that. The Shannons were always an unlucky family, but maybe Ulick'll break the black curse, although I don't know, for he's the very spit and image of his father and able to take his drink like a good one, I can tell ye. This evening he came into McDermott's. There was no one there but meself, it being the high evening, so says he to me:

"'What'll ye have?'

"'Begad, Mr. Shannon,' says I, 'I'll have a pint. And more power to ye, sir!' says I, although I was grinning to meself all the time, for I couldn't help thinking that he was only the son of Henry Shannon, one of the commonest blackguards that ever disgraced this part of the country. You didn't know him, but your mother could tell you about him. You might swear your mother could tell you about him!"

John Brennan did not notice the light of merriment which overspread the face of Shamesy Golliher, for he was looking down towards the hush of the lake, and experiencing a certain feeling of annoyance that this young man should be becoming gradually introduced to him in this way. But Shamesy was still speaking:

"He stood me four pints and two glasses, and nothing would do him when he was going away but he should buy me a whole glass of whiskey. He's what you might call a gay fellow, I can tell you. And God save us! isn't it grand to be that way, even though you never earned it, and not have to be getting your drink like me be nice contriving among the small game of the fields?"

They parted in silence, Shamesy Golliher going eastward towards Garradrimna and John Brennan in the opposite direction and towards his mother's house. His mind had begun to slip into a condition of vacancy when an accident happened to turn it again in the direction of religion. As he came out upon the road he passed a group of children playing between two neighboring houses. The group was made up of the children of two families, the O'Briens and the Vaughans. It was said of Mrs. Vaughan that although she had been married by Father O'Keeffe, and went to Mass every second Sunday, she still clung to the religion into which she had been born. Now her eldest child, a pretty, fair-haired boy, was in the midst of the O'Briens' children. Their mother was what you might call a good woman, for, although she had the most slovenly house along the valley road, she went to Mass as often as Mrs. Brennan. They were making the innocent child repeat phrases out of their prayers and then laughing and mocking him because he could not properly pronounce the long words. They were trying to make him bless himself, but the hands of little Edward could not master the gestures of the formula, and they were jeering at him for his ill-success. When he seemed just upon the verge of tears they began to ask him questions in the answers to which he would seem to have been well trained aforetime, for he repeated them with glibness and enjoyment.

"What religion are ye?"

"I'm a little black Protestant."

"And where will ye go when ye die?"

"I'll go to hell."

"What's hell?"

"A big place bigger than the chapel or the church, with a terrible, grand fire in it."

"And what is it full of?"

"It's full of little fellows like me!"

This was the melancholy piece of catechism John Brennan was constrained to hear as he went past.

It added the last wave of sadness to the gray mood which had been descending upon him by degrees since the beginning of the day.... He stood upon the road and listened for anything in the nature of a sound which might connect his mind with a thought that had some brightness. Although only a few days had elapsed since his return his ears were already beginning to redevelop that delicate perception of slight sounds which comes to one in the quiet places. He now heard a car come through Garradrimna and move a short distance down the valley road. That, he thought, should be Paddy McCann driving the new mistress to her lodging in the house of Sergeant McGoldrick.

The small realization held occupation of his mind as he went into the house of his mother. He was surprised to find that it was past ten. Still lonely as he went to his room, he thought once more of the kind invitation of Mr. Myles Shannon.

CHAPTER VIII

Myles Shannon had ever borne a passionate grudge against Mrs. Brennan. He had loved his brother Henry, and he felt that she, of all people, had had the most powerful hand in instituting the remorse which had hurried him to his doom. Mrs. Brennan, on the other hand, believed firmly that Henry Shannon would have married her, and made of her a decent woman, but for the intervention of his brother Myles. Furthermore, she believed darkly in her heart that the subtle plan of the disastrous "honeymoon" had originated in the brain of Myles, although in this she was wrong. She thought of Henry as being never of that sort. He was wild and mad, with nothing too hot or too heavy for him, but he was not one to concoct schemes. So, when Henry died, Mrs. Brennan had thought well to transmit her hatred of the Shannon family to his brother Myles.

Myles Shannon lived a quiet life there in his big house among the trees upon the side of Scarden, one of the hills which overlooked the valley. In lonely, silent moments he often thought of his brother Henry and of the strange manner in which he had burned out his life. With the end of his brother before him always as a deterrent example, he did not interest himself in women. He interested himself in the business of his cattle and sheep all through each and every day of the year. He did not feel the years slipping past him as he went about his easy, contented life, watching, with great interest, his beef and mutton grow up in the fields.

The cattle in particular stood for the absorbing interest and the one excitement of his life. He looked upon his goings and comings to and from the markets at Dublin and at Wakefield in England as holiday excursions of great enjoyment.

It was during one of his trips to England that he had met Helena Cooper at some hotel in Manchester. He was one to whom the powers of Romance had remained strangers, yet now, when they at last came into his life, it was with a force that carried away all the protection of his mind. He wanted some one to fill the loneliness of the big house on Scarden Hill, and so he set his heart upon Helena Cooper.

He returned to the valley a different man. Quite suddenly he began to have a greater interest in his appearance, and it was noticed that he grew sentimental and became easy in his dealings. It began to be whispered around that, even so late in life, almost at the close of the middle period which surely marks the end of a man's prime, Myles Shannon had fallen in love and was about to be married.

It was a notable rumor, and although it was fifteen years since the death of Henry Shannon, Mrs. Brennan, as one having a good reason to be interested in the affairs of the Shannon family, became excited.

"Indeed it was high time for him to think of it," she said to a neighbor one Sunday morning, "before he turned into a real ould blackguard of a bachelor—and who d'ye say the girl is?"

"Why, then, they say she's an English lady, and that she's grand and young."

Mrs. Brennan was a great one for "ferreting-out" things. Once she had set her mind upon knowing a thing, there was little possibility of preventing her. And now she was most anxious to know whom Myles Shannon was about to marry. So when she saw the old bent postmistress taking the air upon the valley road later on in the day she brought her into the sewing-room and, over a cup of tea, proceeded to satisfy her curiosity.

"There must be letters?" she said after they had come round to a discussion of the rumored marriage.

"Oh, yes, indeed. There's letters coming and going, coming and going," the old lady wheezed. "A nice-looking ould codger, isn't he, to be writing letters to a young girl?"

"And how d'ye know she's young?"

"How do I know, is it, how do I know? Well, well, isn't that my business? To know and to mind."

"You're a great woman."

"I do my duty, that's all, Mrs. Brennan, as sure as you're there. And d'ye imagine for a moment I was going to let Myles Shannon pass, for all he's such a great swank of a farmer? She *is* a young girl."

"Well, well?"

"There's no reason to misdoubt me in the least, for I saw her photo and it coming through the post."

"A big, enlarged photo, I suppose?"

"Aye, the photo of a young girl in her bloom."

"I suppose she's very nice?"

"She's lovely, and 'tis what I said to myself as I looked upon her face, that it would be the pity of the world to see her married to a middling ould fellow like Myles Shannon."

"And I suppose, now, that she has a nice name?"

"Aye. It is that. And what you might call a grand name."

A long pause now fell between the two women, as if both were endeavoring to form in their minds some great resolve to which their hearts were prompting them. The old postmistress delivered her next speech in a whisper:

"Her name is Helena Cooper, and her address is 15 Medway Avenue, Manchester!"

The two women now nudged one another in simultaneous delight. Mrs. Brennan ran the direction over and over in her mind as if suddenly fearful that some dreadful stroke of forgetfulness might come to overthrow her chance of revenge upon her false, dead lover through the great injury she now contemplated doing to his brother.... She made an excuse of going to the kitchen to put more water upon the teapot and, when she went there, scribbled the name and address upon the wall beside the fireplace.

When she returned to the sewing-room the old postmistress was using her handkerchief to hide the smile of satisfaction which was dancing around her mouth. She knew what was just presently running through Mrs. Brennan's mind, and she was glad and thankful that she herself was about to be saved the trouble of writing to Miss Cooper.... Her hand was beginning to be quavery and incapable of writing a hard, vindictive letter. Besides that Mr. Shannon was an influential man in the district, and the Post Office was not above suspicion. She was thankful to Mrs. Brennan now, and said the tea was nice, very nice.

Yet, immediately that the information, for which she had hungered since the rumor of Myles Shannon's marriage began to go the rounds, was in her keeping, Mrs. Brennan ceased to display any unusual interest in the old, bespectacled maid. Nor did the postmistress continue to be excited by the friendly presence of Mrs. Brennan, for she, on her part, was immensely pleased and considered that the afternoon had attained to a remarkable degree of success.... From what she had read of her productions passing through the post, she knew that Mrs. Brennan was the woman who could write the strong, poisonous letter. Besides, who had a better right to be writing it—about one of the Shannon family?

Soon she was going out the door and down the white road towards Garradrimna.... Now wasn't Mrs. Brennan the anxious and the prompt woman; she would be writing to Miss Cooper this very evening?... As she went she met young couples on bicycles passing to distant places through the fragrant evening. The glamor of Romance seemed to hang around them.

"Now isn't that the quare way for them to be spending the Sabbath?" she said to herself as she hobbled along.

The Angelus was just beginning to ring out across the waving fields with its sweet, clear sound as Mrs. Brennan regained the sewing-room after having seen her visitor to the door, but, good woman though she was, she did not stop to answer its holy summons. Her mind was driving her relentlessly towards the achievement of her intention. The pen was already in her hand, and she was beginning to scratch out "a full account," as she termed it, of Mr. Myles Shannon for the benefit of Miss Helena Cooper, whoever she might be. Through page after page she continued her attack while the fire of her hate was still burning brightly through her will.

It had been her immemorial custom to send full accounts abroad whenever one of the valley dwellers made attempts at assertion, but not one of the Shannons had so far offered her such a golden opportunity. For the moment she was in her glory.

She announced herself as a good friend of this girl, whose name she had only heard just now. She wrote that she would not like to see Miss Cooper deceived by a man she had no opportunity of knowing in his real character, such as Mr. Shannon.

Now it was a fact that Myles, unlike his brother Henry, had not been a notable antagonist of the Commandments. It was true, of course, that he was not distinguished for the purity of his ways when he went adventuring about the bye-ways of Dublin after a day at the cattle market, and people from the valley, cropping up most unexpectedly, had witnessed some of his exploits and had sent magnified stories winging afar. But he had ruined no girl, and was even admirable in his habits when at home in his lonely house among the trees.

This, however, was not the Mr. Shannon that Mrs. Brennan set down in her letter to Helena Cooper. It was rather the portrait of his brother Henry, the wild libertine, that she painted, for, in the high moments of her hate, she was as one blinded by the ecstasy that had come upon her. The name of Shannon held for her only one significance, and, for the moment, it was an abysmal vision which dazzled her eyes.

Soon there came a communication from Miss Cooper to Mr. Shannon which had the effect of nipping his green romance while it was still young.... It asked him was this true and was that true?... The easy, sentimental way he had looked upon the matter was suddenly kindled into a deeper feeling, and he thought of having the girl now at all costs.... He wrote a fine reply in justification. It was a clear, straight piece of writing, and, although it pained him greatly, he was compelled to admit that the statements about which Miss

Cooper wished to be satisfied were no more than the truth in relation to a certain member of the Shannon family. But they related to his dead brother Henry and not to him.... He prayed the forgiveness of forgetfulness for the dead.... He volunteered the production of convincing proof for every statement here made in regard to himself.

But the old lady at the Post Office had something to say in the matter. She had read Miss Cooper's letter, and as she now read the letter of Mr. Shannon she knew that should it reach her this girl must be fully satisfied as to his character, for his was a fine piece of pleading.... But she could not let Mrs. Brennan have all the secret satisfaction for the destruction of his love-affair. The bitter woman in the valley had done the ugly, obvious part of the work, but she was in a position to hurry it to secret, deadly completion.... So that evening the letter, which it had given Myles Shannon such torture to write, was burned at the fire in the kitchen behind the Post Office.... He wrote to Helena Cooper again and yet again, but the same thing happened.... His third letter had turned purely pathetic in its tone. The old lady said to herself that it made her laugh like anything.

At last he fell to considering that her affection for him could not have been very deep seeing that she had allowed it to be so strongly influenced by some poisonous letter from an anonymous enemy.... Yet there were moments when he knew that he could never forget her nor escape, through all the years he might live, from the grand dream her first tenderness had raised up in his heart. In its immediate aspect he was a little angry that the rumor of a contemplated marriage on his part should have gone abroad. But he had almost triumphed over this slight feeling of annoyance when there came to him, some month later, the "account" that had been written about him to Miss Cooper without a word of comment enclosed.... The old lady at the office had seen to that, for the letter accompanying it as far as Garradrimna had gone the way of Mr. Shannon's letters.... This had made her laugh also with its note of wonder as to why he had made no attempt to explain.... If only he would say that the statements made against him were all mere lies. Of course she did not believe a word of them, but she wished him to say so in a letter to her.... The Post Office was saved from suspicion by this second bit of destruction, although it had done its work well.

The bare, scurrilous note caused a blaze of indignation turning to hatred to take possession of his soul which had hitherto been largely distinguished by kindly influences. He had his suspicions at once that it was the work of Mrs. Brennan.

There was a letter of hers locked in a bureau in the parlor with other things which had been the property of his dead brother Henry. They were all sad things which related intimately to the queer life he had led. This old faded letter from Nan Byrne was the one she had written asking him for Christ's sake to marry her, now that she felt her misfortune coming upon her.... A hard look came into his eyes as he began to compare the weak handwriting. Yes, it was hers surely, beyond a shadow of doubt.... He locked this thing which had so changed the course of his life with the things of his brother.

It was queer, he thought, that she, of all people, who should be prone to silence, had thought fit, after the passage of so many years, to meddle with dead things in the hope of ending other dreams which, until now, had lived brightly. He continued to brood himself into bitter determinations. He resolved that, as no other girl had come greatly into his life before the coming of Helena Cooper, no other one must enter now that she was gone. She was gone, and must the final disaster of his affections narrow down to a mere piece of sentimental renunciation? Strange, contradictory attitudes built themselves up in his mind.

Out of his brooding there grew before him the structure of a plan. This woman had besmirched his brother, helping him towards the destruction of his life, for it was in this light, as a brother, he had viewed the matter always; and now, in her attempt to besmirch himself, she had spoiled his dream. He had grown angry after the slow fashion which was the way of his thought, but his resolve was now sure and deliberate.

There was her son! He had just gone to some kind of college in England to prepare for the priesthood, and the antecedents of a priest must be without blemish. It was not the youth's fault, but his mother was Nan Byrne, and some one must pay.... And why should she desire to bring punishment of any kind upon him for his brother's sin with her? He had loved his brother, and it was only natural to think that she loved her son. And through that love might come the desolation of her heart. To allow the blossom to brighten in her eye and then, suddenly, to wither it at a blast. To permit this John Brennan to approach the sacred portals of the priesthood and then to cause him to be cast adrift.

The thought of how he might put a more delicate turn to the execution of his plan had come to him as he journeyed down from Dublin with John Brennan. He knew that his nephew, Ulick, had lived the rather reckless student life of Dublin. Just recently he had been drawing him out. But he was no weakling, and it was not possible that any of those ways might yet submerge him. However, his influence acting upon a weaker mind might have effect and produce again the degenerate that had not fully leaped to life in him. If he were brought into contact with John Brennan it might be the means of effecting, in a less direct way, the result which must be obtained.

It was with this thought simmering in his brain that Myles Shannon had invited John Brennan to the friendship and company of his nephew. When he had spoken of the Great War it was the condition of his own mind that had prompted the thought, for it was filled with the impulse of destruction.

CHAPTER IX

It is on his passage through the village of Garradrimna that we may most truly observe John Brennan, in sharp contrast with his dingy environment, as he goes to hear morning Mass at the instigation of his mother, whose pathetic fancy fails to picture him in any other connection. It is a beautiful morning, and the sun is already high. There is a clean freshness upon all things. The tall trees which form a redeeming background for the uneven line of the ugly houses on the western side of the street are flinging their rich raiment wildly upon the light breeze where it floats like the decorative garments of a ballet dancer. The light winds are whipping the lightness of the morning.

The men of drink are already stirring about in anticipation. Hubert Manning is striking upon the door of Flynn's, the grocery establishment, which, in the heavy blindness of his thirst, he takes to be one of the seven publichouses of Garradrimna. He is running about like some purged sinner, losing patience at last hard by the Gate of Heaven. In the course of her inclusive chronicles his mother had told John Brennan the life history of Hubert Manning. For sixty odd years he had bent his body in hard battle with the clay, until the doubtful benefit of a legacy had come to change the current of his life. The fortune, with its sudden diversion towards idleness and enjoyment, had caused all the latent villainy of the man, which the soil had subdued, to burst forth with violence. He was now a drunken old cur whom Sergeant McGoldrick caused to spend a fortune in fines.

"Just imagine the people who do be left the money!" said Mrs. Brennan, as she told the story.

John Brennan passes on. He meets the bill-poster, Thomas James. His dark, red face displays an immense anxiety. He is going for his first pint with a pinch of salt held most carefully in his hand. His present condition is a fact to be deplored, for he was famous in his time and held the record in Garradrimna for fast drinking of a pint. He could drink twenty pints in a day. Hence his decline and the pinch of salt now held so carefully in his hand. This is to keep down the first pint, and if the operation be safely effected it is quite possible that the other nineteen will give him no trouble.

Coming in the valley road are Shamesy Golliher and Martin Connell. In the distance they appear as small, shrinking figures, moving in abasement beneath the Gothic arches of the elms. They represent the advance guard of those who leave the sunlit fields on a summer morning to come into the dark, cavernous pubs of Garradrimna.

On the side of the street, distant from that upon which John Brennan is walking, moves the famous figure of Padna Padna, slipping along like some spirit of discontent and immortal longing, doomed forever to wander. He mistakes the student for one of the priests and salutes him by tipping his great hat lightly with his little fore-finger.

And here comes yet another, this one with speed and determination in his stride, for it is Anthony Shaughness, who has spent three-fourths of his life running away from Death.

"Will you save a life; will you save a life?" he whispers wildly, clutching John by the arm. "I have a penny, but sure a penny is no good, sir; and I want tuppence-ha'penny to add to it for the price of a pint; but sure you won't mind when it's to save my life! I know you'll give it to me for the love of God!"

This is a very well-known request in the mouth of Anthony Shaughness, and John Brennan has attended it so very often during the past few years as to deserve a medal for life-saving. Yet he now takes the coppers from his small store of pocket-money and gives them to the dipsomaniac, who moves rapidly in the direction of "The World's End."

There is presently an exciting interlude. They are just opening up at Brannagan's as he goes past. The sleepy-looking barmaid has come to the newly-opened door, and makes an ungraceful gesture in gathering up her ugly dishevelled hair. A lout of a lad with a dirty cigarette in his mouth appears suddenly. They begin to grin at one another in foolish rapture, for it is a lovers' meeting. Through the doorway at which they stand the smell of stale porter is already assaulting the freshness of the morning. They enter the bar surreptitiously and John Brennan can hear the swish of a pint in the glass in which it is being filled. The usual morning gift, he thinks, with which this maiden favors this gallant lover of a new Romance.... There comes to him suddenly the idea that his name has been mentioned in this dark place just now.... He goes on walking quickly towards the chapel.

The plan which Myles Shannon had originated was not lacking in subtlety. He foresaw a certain clash of character, between his nephew and the son of Nan Byrne, which must become most interesting as he watched it out of his malevolence. He could never, never, forget what she had done.... And always, beyond the desolation which appeared from concentration of his revengeful intentions, he beheld the ruins of her son.

He often thought it puzzling how she should never have imagined that some one like him might be tempted to do at some time what he was now about to do. It seemed remarkable beyond all else that her mind should possess such an opaque oneness of purpose, such an extraordinary "thickness," to use the term of the valley.

Yet this was a quality peculiar to the gentle hush of the grassy places. It seemed to arise from the removal of an intelligent feeling of humanity from the conduct of life and the replacement of it by a spitefulness that killed and blinded. It was the explanation of many of the tragedies of the valley. Like a malignant wind, it warped the human growth within the valley's confines. It was what had happened to Mrs. Brennan and, because of the action he was taking in regard to her, what was now about to happen to Myles Shannon. He seemed to forget, as he went about his vengeance, that subtlety is akin to humor, and that humor, in its application to the satiric perception of things, is the quality which constantly heals the cut it has made. He might certainly leave the mark of his vengeance upon Mrs. Brennan, but there was the danger of the weapon recoiling upon himself and his kinsman. It was a horrible plan indeed, this, of setting one young man to ruin another. It was such a conflict, with such an anticipated ending, as had shaped itself inevitably out of the life of the valley. Where life was an endless battle of conflicting characters and antagonized dispositions it seemed particularly meet that a monumental conflict should at last have been instituted.

Ulick Shannon was finding the valley very little to his mind. But for the intervention of his uncle he was several times upon the point of returning to Dublin. Although it was for a rest he had come the place was too damnably dull. Garradrimna was an infernal hole! Yet he went there often, and it was remarkable that his uncle said never a word when he arrived home from the village, several nights, in a condition that was not one of absolute sobriety. On the contrary, he seemed to take a certain joyful interest in such happenings. His uncle often spoke of the young man, John Brennan, whom he desired him to meet, and it was surprising that this young man had not made the visit he had promised to the house among the trees.

Myles Shannon was beginning to be annoyed by the appearance of this slight obstruction in the path of his plan. Had Mrs. Brennan forbidden the friendship he had proposed? It was very like her indeed, and of course she had her reasons.... But it would never do to let her triumph over him now, and he having such a lovely plan. He would go so far as to send his nephew to call at her house to make the acquaintance of Nan Byrne's son. It would be queer surely to see him calling at that house and inquiring for John Brennan when his father had gone there aforetime to see John Brennan's mother. But how was Ulick to know and view from such an angle this aspect of his existence?

Yet, after all, the meeting of John Brennan and Ulick Shannon happened quite accidentally and upon such a morning as we have seen John in Garradrimna.

Ulick had gone for a walk around that way before his breakfast. He was not feeling particularly well as he paused at the end of the valley road to survey the mean street of Garradrimna, down which he had marched last night with many a wild thought rushing into his mind as the place and the people fell far beneath his high gaze.

His quick eye caught sight of something now which seemed a curiously striking piece in the drab mosaic of his morning. It was a little party of four going towards the chapel. The pair in front could possibly be none other than the bridegroom and his bride. It was easy to see that marriage was their purpose from the look of open rapture upon their faces. The bridesmaid and the best man were laughing and chatting gaily as they walked behind them. They seemed to be having the best of it.

Ulick thought it interesting to see this pair moving eagerly towards a mysterious purpose.... He was struck by the fact that it was a most merciful thing that all men do not lift the veil of life so early as he had done.... The harsh, slight laugh which came from him was like the remembered laughter of a dead man.

Now that his eyes were falling, with an unfilled look, upon the street along which the four had gone he began to see people who had been looking out move away from the squinting windows and a few seconds later come hurriedly out of their houses and go towards the chapel.

The poor, self-conscious clod, who had dearly desired to marry the girl of his fancy quietly and with no prying eyes, amid the fragrance of the fine June morning, had, after all, succeeded only in drawing about him the leering attention of all the village. There were ever so many people going towards the chapel this morning. The lot was large enough to remind one of a Sunday congregation at either Mass, this black drove now moving up the laneway. Ulick Shannon went forward to join it.

Coming near the chapel he encountered a young man in black, who wore the look of a student. This must be John Brennan, he thought, of whom his uncle had so repeatedly spoken. He turned and said:

"Good morning! I'm Ulick Shannon, and I fancy you're Brennan, the chap my uncle has talked of so often. He has been expecting you to call at Scarden House."

They shook hands.

"Yes, I'm John Brennan, and I'm delighted to meet you. I have not forgotten your uncle's kind invitation."

Together they entered the House of God.... Father O'Keeffe was already engaged in uniting the couple. Distantly they could hear him mumbling the words of the ceremony.... All eyes were upon the priest and the four people at the altar.... Suddenly Ulick giggled openly, and John Brennan blushed in confusion, for this was irreverence such as he had never before experienced in the presence of sacred things.

CHAPTER X

Next day Ulick Shannon made a call upon John Brennan and invited him for a drive. Outside upon the road Charlie Clarke's motor was snorting and humming. Ulick had learned to drive a car in Dublin, and had now hired Mr. Clarke's machine for the day.

"You see," he said airily, "that I have dispensed with the sanctimonious Charlie and am driving myself. Meaning no respect to you, Brennan, one approach to a priest is as much as I can put up with at a time."

Mrs. Brennan had come to the window, which looked out upon the little garden wicket by which they were standing.... Her eyes were dancing and wild thoughts were rushing into her mind.... Here, at last, was the achieved disaster and the sight her eyes had most dreaded to see—her son and the son of Henry Shannon talking together as brothers.

An ache that was akin to hunger seemed to have suddenly attacked her. Her lips became parched and dry and her jaws went through the actions of swallowing although there was nothing in her mouth. Then she felt herself being altogether obliterated as she stood there by the window. She was like a wounded bird that had broken itself in an attempt to attain to the sunlight beyond.... And to think that it had fallen at last, this shadow of separation from her lovely son. John came to the door and called in:

"I'm going for a drive in the motor with Mr. Shannon, mother."

These were his very words, and they caused her to move away towards the sewing-room with the big tears gathering into her eyes. From her seat she saw her son take up his proud position by the side of Ulick Shannon. There was something for you, now! Her son driving in a motor car with a young man who was going on to be a doctor, in the high noon of a working day, all down through the valley of Tullahanogue. If only it happened to be with any other one in the whole world. What would all the people say but what they must say?... She saw the two students laughing just before the car started as if some joke had suddenly leaped into being between them.

Ned Brennan came into the room. He had been making an effort to do something in the garden when the car had distracted him from his task. Well, that was what you might call a grand thing! While he was here digging in his drought, his son, I thank ye, going off to drive in a motor with a kind of a gentleman. His mind went swiftly moving towards a white heat of temper which must be eventually cooled in the black pools of Garradrimna. He came into the room, a great blast of a man in his anger, his boots heavy with the clay of the garden.

"Well, be the Holy Farmer! that's the grand turn-out!... But sure they're a kind of connections, don't you know, and I suppose 'tis only natural?"

Great God! He had returned again to this, and to the words she feared most of all to hear falling from his mouth.

"A curious attraction, don't you know, that the breed of the Byrnes always had for the breed of the Shannons. Eh, Nan?"

Mrs. Brennan said nothing. It had been the way with her that she felt a certain horror of Ned when he came to her in this state, but now she was being moved by a totally different feeling. She was not without a kind of pity for him as she suddenly realized once more how she had done him a terrible and enduring injury.... As he stood there glowering down upon her he was of immense bulk and significance. If he struck her now she would not mind in the least.

"And they're like one another too, them two chaps, as like as brothers. And mebbe they are brothers. Eh, Nan, eh; what happened the child you had for Henry Shannon? It died, did it? Why 'tis only the other night that Larry Cully came at me again about it in Garradrimna. 'I see you have your sons home about you,' says he, 'and that must be the great comfort to a man, your son John,' says he, 'and your son Ulick. Maybe ye never heard tell,' says he, 'that Grace Gogarty's child died young and that Henry Shannon bought his other son from his other mother-in-law to prevent it being a rising disgrace to him. Bought it for a small sum,' says he, 'and put it in the place of his lawful son, and his wife never suspected anything until the day she died, poor woman; for she was to be pitied, having married such a blackguard.' Is that true, is it, Nan?"

Oh, Blessed Mother! this was even more terrible than the suspicion Marse Prendergast had put upon her. It seemed less of a crime that the little innocent babe should have been murdered in this house and buried in the garden than that her old, dead mother should have sold it to Henry Shannon. And how was she to know? Twenty-five years had passed since that time when she had been at Death's door, nor realizing anything.... And her mother had never told her.... It would be strange if she had gone digging at any time for the tiny bones of the little infant that had never been baptized. People passing the road might suspect her purpose and say hard things.... But sure they said hard things of her still after all the years. It was dreadful to think how any one could concoct a lie like this, and that no one could forget. Old Marse Prendergast knew well. Deep in her wicked mind, for twenty-five years, the secret had been hidden. It was a torture to think of the way she would be hinting at it forever.... And just quite recently she had threatened to tell John.

Bit by bit was being erected in her mind the terrible speculation as to what really was the truth and the full extent of her sin. Yet it was not a thing she could set about making inquiries after.... She wondered and wondered did Myles Shannon, the uncle of Ulick, know the full truth. Why did not her husband drop that grimy, powerful hand? Her breasts craved its blow now, even as they had yearned long ago for the fumbling of the little, blind mouth.

But he was merely asking her for money to buy drink for himself in Garradrimna. Hitherto this request had always given her pain, but now, somehow, it came differently to her ears. There was no hesitation on her part, no making of excuses. She went upstairs to the box which held her most dear possession—the money she had saved so well through all the years for the fitting-out of Ned to go proudly with her to attend the ordination of their son John. She opened the box with the air of one doing a deliberate thing. The money, which amounted in all to about five pounds, was still in the form in which she had managed to scrape it together. In notes and gold and silver, and even copper. Before this it would have appeared as a sacrilege on her part to have touched a penny of it, but now she had no thought of this kind. Ned wanted the money to purchase the means of forgetfulness of the great injury she had done him.

She counted thirty pennies, one by one, into the pocket of her apron. This seemed the least suspicious way of giving it to him, for he had still no idea that she could have any little store laid by. It was hardly possible when one considered how much he drank upon her in the village.

She came down the stairs in silence, and spoke no word to him as she handed over the money. His lips seemed to split into a sort of sneer as he took it from her. Then he went out the door quickly and down the white road toward Garradrimna.

For the admiration and surprise of John Brennan, Ulick Shannon had been displaying his skill with the wheel. Soon the white, tidy houses beyond the valley were whizzing past and they were running down the easy road which led into the village of Ballinamult. They had moved in a continuous cloud of dust from Tullahanogue.

Ulick said he was choked with dust as he brought the car to a standstill outside the "North Leinster Arms." He marched deliberately into the public bar, and John Brennan followed after with less sure footsteps, for it was his first appearance in a place of this kind. There was a little, plump girl standing up on a chair rearranging the bottles of whiskey and dusting the shelves.

Ulick would seem to have already visited this tavern, for he addressed the girl rather familiarly as "Mary Essie." She looked at the young man impudently as she wheeled around to exhibit herself to the best advantage. Ulick leaned his elbows upon the low counter and gazed towards her with his deep, dark eyes. Some quite unaccountable thing caused John Brennan to blush, but he noticed that the girl was not blushing. She was more brazenly forcing her body into exhibition.

Ulick called for a drink, whatever his friend Brennan would have, and a bottle of Bass for himself. It appeared a little wrong to John that he should be about to partake of a drink in a pub., for the "North Leinster Arms" was nothing more than a sufficiently bad public-house. He had a sudden recollection of having once been given cakes and sweets in an evil-smelling tap-room one day he had gone with his mother long ago to Mullaghowen. He thought of the kind of wine he had been given that day and immediately the name was forced to his lips by the thought—"Port wine!"

When the barmaid turned around to fill their drinks the young men had a view of the curves of her body. John Brennan was surprised to find himself dwelling upon them in the intense way of his friend.

Before they left Ulick had many drinks of various kinds, and it was interesting to observe how he expanded with their influence. He began to tell "smutty" stories to Mary Essie. She listened with attention. No blush came into her face, and her glad neck looked brazen.... John Brennan felt himself swallowing great gulps of disgust.... His training had led him to associate the female form with the angelic form coming down from Heaven. Yet here was something utterly different.... A vulgar girl, with fat, round hands and big breasts, her lips red as a recent wound in soft flesh, and looking lonely.

He was glad when they regained the sunlight, yet the day was of such a character as creates oppression by the very height of its splendor. Ulick was in such a mood for talk that they had almost forgotten the luncheon-basket at the back of the car.

Beyond Ballinamult they stopped again where the ruins of a moldering Abbey lay quietly surrounded by a circle of furze-covered hills.... Ulick expanded still further with the meal, yet his discourse still ran along the old trail. He was favoring his friend with a sketch of his life, and it seemed to be made up largely of the women he had known in Dublin. Quite suddenly he said what seemed to John a very terrible thing:

"I have learned a lot from them, and let me tell you this—it has been my experience that you could not trust your own mother or the girl of your heart. They seem to lack control, even the control of religion. They do not realize religion at all. They are creatures of impulse."

Here was a sentiment that questioned the very fact of existence.... It seemed dreadful to connect the triumph of love and devotion that was his mother with this consequent suggestion of the failure of existence.... Together they went across the grassy distance towards the crumbling ruin wherein the good monks of old had lived and prayed. And surely, he thought, the great spirit of holiness which had led men hither to spend their lives in penance and good works could not have departed finally from this quiet place, nor from the green fields beyond the rim of furze-covered hills.

Yet upon his ears were falling the even, convincing tones of Ulick Shannon, still speaking cynically.

"Behold," he was saying, "that it is to this place the younger generation throng on the Sabbath. Around you, upon the ruined and bare walls, you will observe not pious words, but the coupled names of those who have come here to sin."

"And look at this!" he exclaimed, picking from a niche in the wall a long shin bone of one of the ancient monks, which possessed the reputed power of cures and miracles. For a moment he examined it with a professional eye, then handed it to John Brennan. There were two names scribbled upon it in pencil, and beneath them a lewd expression. Ulick had only laid hands upon it by the merest accident, but it immediately gave body to all the airy ideas he had been putting forth. There was something so greatly irreverent in the appearance of this accidental piece of evidence that no argument could be put forward against it. It was terrible and conclusive.

The evening was far advanced when John Brennan returned home. His mother and father were seated in the kitchen. His father was drunk, and she was reading him a holy story, with an immeasurable feeling of despondence in her tones. John became aware of this as he entered the house.

CHAPTER XI

Rebecca Kerr had been ill for a few days and did not attend school until the Monday following her arrival in the valley. There she made the acquaintance of Mrs. Wyse, the principal of Tullahanogue Girls' School, and Monica McKeon, the assistant of Tullahanogue Boys' School. Mrs. Wyse was a woman who divided her energies between the education of other women's children and the production of children of her own. Year by year, and with her growing family, had her life narrowed down to the painful confines of its present condition. She had the reputation of being a hard mistress to the children and a harsh superior to her assistants. From the very first she seemed anxious to show her authority over Rebecca Kerr.

In the forenoon of this day she was standing by her blackboard at the east end of the school, imparting some history to her most advanced class. Rebecca was at the opposite end teaching elementary arithmetic to the younger children when something in the would-be impressive seriousness of her principal's tone caused her to smile openly.

Mrs. Wyse saw the smile, and it lit her anger. She called loudly:

"Miss Kerr, are you quite sure that that exercise in simple addition is correct?"

"Yes, perfectly certain, Mrs. Wyse."

The chalk had slipped upon the greasy blackboard, making a certain 5 to appear as a 6 from the distance at which she stood, and it was into this accidental trap that Mrs. Wyse had fallen. Previous assistants had studied her ways and had given up the mistake of contradicting her even when she was obviously in the wrong. But this was such a straight issue, and Rebecca Kerr had had no opportunity of knowing her. She came down in a flaming temper from the rostrum. Rebecca awaited her near approach with a smiling and assured complacency which must have been maddening. But Mrs. Wyse was not one to admit a mistake. Quick as lightning she struck upon the complaint that the exercise was beyond the course of instruction scheduled for this particular standard.... And here were the foundations of an enmity laid between these two women. They would not be friends in any fine way through the length of all the long days they might teach together.

Thus for Rebecca the first day in the valley school dragged out its slow length and was dreary and dreadful until noon. Then Monica McKeon came in from the Boys' School and they took their luncheon together.... They went on chattering away until the door of the schoolroom was suddenly darkened by the shadows of two men. The three women arose in confusion as Master Donnellan called them to the door. There was a young man standing outside who presented a strong contrast to the venerable figure of the master. The latter, in his roundabout, pedagogic way, went on to tell how the stranger had strayed into the school playground and made himself known. He wished to show him the whole of the building, and introduced him as "Mr. Ulick Shannon, Mr. Myles Shannon's nephew, you know."

The three female teachers took an immediate mental note of the young man. They saw him as neat and well-dressed, with a half-thoughtful, half-reckless expression upon his fine face, with its deep-set, romantic eyes. The few words he spoke during the general introduction appeared to Rebecca to be in such a gentle voice. There were some moments of awkward silence. Then, between the five of them, they managed to say a few conventional things. All the while those great, deep eyes seemed to be set upon Rebecca, and she was experiencing the disquieting feeling that she had met him at some previous time in some other place in this wide world. The eyes of Monica McKeon were upon both of them in a way that seemed an attempt to search their minds for their thoughts of the moment.

Immediately he was gone Mrs. Wyse and Miss McKeon fell to talking of him:

"He's the hateful-looking thing; I'd hate him like poison," said Monica.

"Indeed what could he be and the kind of a father he had? Sure I remember him well, a quare character," said Mrs. Wyse.

"I wonder what could have brought him around here to-day of all days since he came to Scarden?"

This with her eyes set firmly upon Rebecca.

Mrs. Wyse was not slow to pick up the insinuation.

"Oh, looking after fresh girls always, the same as his father."

"He's not bad-looking."

"No; but wouldn't you know well he has himself destroyed with the kind of life he lives up in Dublin? They say he's gone to the bad and that he'll never pass his exams."

Every word of the conversation seemed to be spoken with the direct intention of attacking certain feelings which had already begun to rise in the breast of Rebecca Kerr.... Her mind was being held fast by the well-remembered spell of his eyes.

The afternoon passed swiftly for Mrs. Wyse. She was so engrossed by thought of this small thing that had happened that she gave wrong dates in another history lesson, false notes in the music lesson, and more than one incorrect answer to simple sums in the arithmetic lesson.

Rebecca was glad when three o'clock and her freedom at last came. Out in the sunlight she would be able to indulge in certain realizations which were impossible of enjoyment here in this crowded schoolroom. The day was still enthroned beneath the azure dome. This was the period of its languorous yawn when it seemed to dream for a space and gather strength before it came down from its high place and went into the long, winding ways of evening.

There were men engaged in raising sand from a pit by the roadside as she passed along. A pause in the ringing of their shovels made her conscious that they had stopped in their labor to gaze after her as she went.... Her neck was warm and blushing beneath the shadow of her hair.

Her confusion extended to every portion of her body when she came upon Ulick Shannon around a bend of the road, book in hand, sauntering along.

He saluted as she overtook him, and spoke of the pleasant afternoon.... She hoped he was enjoying his holidays here in the valley. He seemed to be spending the time very quietly. Reading? Poetry? Just fancy! *The Daffodil Fields*, by John Masefield. What a pretty name! Was he devoted to poetry, and was this particular poem a good one?

"It is a great tale of love and passion that happened in one of the quiet places of the world," he told her with a kind of enthusiasm coming into his words for the first time.

"One of the quiet places?" she murmured, evidently at a loss for something else to say.

"Yes, a quiet place which must have been like this place and yet, at the same time, most wonderfully different, for no poet at all could imagine any tale of love and passion springing from the life about us here. The people of the valley seem to have died before they were born. I will lend you this poem, if you'd care to have it."

"Oh, thank you, Mr. Shannon!" she said.

They had wandered down a lane which led from the high road towards the peaceful fields beyond the little lake. This lane, he told her, was called "The Road of the Dead," and would afford her a short cut to her lodging at Sergeant McGoldrick's.

For lack of anything else to say, she remarked upon the strangeness of this name—The Road of the Dead. He said it seemed a title particularly suitable. He went on to elaborate the idea he had just expressed:

"Around and about here they are all dead—dead. No passion of any kind comes to light their existence. Their life is a thing done meanly, shudderingly within the shadow of the grave. That is how I have been seeing it for the past few weeks. They hate the occurrence of new people in their midst. They hate me already, and now they will hate you. The sight of us walking together like this must surely cause them to hate us still more."

She was wondering that his words should hold a sense of consideration for her, seeing that they had been acquainted only such a short while.

"This way leads from a graveyard to a graveyard, and they have a silly superstition that dead couples are sometimes seen walking here. Particularly dismal also do I consider this picture of their imagination. The idea of any one thinking us a dead couple!"

As he said this her blushing cheek showed certainly that life was strong in her.... Upon the wings of his words grand thoughts had gone flying through her mind. All day she had been looking forward with dread to the yellow, sickly, sunlit time after school. And now to think that the miracle of this romantic young man had happened.... Both grew silent. Rebecca's eyes were filling with visions and wandering over a field of young green corn. They were dancing upon the waves of sunlight which shimmered over all the clean, feathery surface of the field. The eyes of Ulick were straying from the landscape and dwelling upon her deeply, upon the curves of her throat and bosom, and upon the gentle billows of her hair. Over all his face was clouding that mysterious, murky expression which had come as he gazed upon the little barmaid of the "North Leinster Arms" a few days previously.

CHAPTER XII

Rebecca wanted some light blouses. Those she possessed had survived through one summer, and it was all that could be expected of them. So one day she ran down to Brennan's, during the half hour allowed for recreation, to leave the order. When she entered the sewing-room Mrs. Brennan was busy at her machine. Her ever-tired eyes struggled into a beaming look upon Rebecca.

The young girl, with her rich body, seemed to bring a clean freshness into the room. For a moment the heavy smell of the miscellaneous materials about her died down in the nostrils of Mrs. Brennan. But this might have arisen from a lapse of other faculties occasioned by her agreeable surprise. So here was the new teacher who had so recently occupied her tongue to such an extent. She now beheld her hungrily.

Rebecca laid her small parcel of muslin upon the table, and became seated at the request of Mrs. Brennan.

"That's the grand day, ma'am," said she.

"'Tis the grand day indeed, miss," said Mrs. Brennan.

"Not nice, however, to be in a stuffy schoolroom."

"Indeed you might swear that, especially in such a school as Tullahanogue, with a woman like Mrs. Wyse; she's the nice-looking article of a mistress!"

Rebecca almost bounded in her chair. She had fancied Mrs. Brennan, from the nature of her occupation, as a gabster, but she had not reckoned upon such a sudden and emphatic confirmation of her notion. Immediately she tried to keep the conversation from taking this turn, which, in a way, might bring it to a personal issue. But Mrs. Brennan was not to be baulked of her opportunity.

She began to favor her visitor with a biography of Mrs. Wyse. It was a comprehensive study, including all her aspects and phases. Her father and his exact character, and her mother and what she was. Her husband, and how the marriage had been arranged. How she had managed to gain her position. Everything was explained with a wealth of detail.

Rebecca out of the haze into which the garrulous recital had led her, spoke suddenly and reminded Mrs. Brennan of the passage of the half hour. Mrs. Brennan quickly fancied that the cause of the girl's lack of enthusiasm in this outpouring of information might have arisen from the fact that Mrs. Wyse had forestalled her with a previous attack. Thus, by a piece of swift transition, she must turn the light upon herself and upon the far, bright period of her young girlhood.

Now maybe Miss Kerr would like to look through the album of photos upon the table. This was a usual extension of feminine curiosity.... Rebecca opened the heavy, embossed album and began to turn over the pages.... There was a photo of a young girl near the beginning. She was of considerable beauty, even so far as could be discerned from this faded photo, taken in the early eighties. As Rebecca lingered over it, the face of Mrs. Brennan was lit by a sad smile.

"She was nice, and who might she have been?" said Rebecca.

"That was me when I was little and innocent," said Mrs. Brennan.

Rebecca looked from Mrs. Brennan to the photo, and again from the photo to Mrs. Brennan. She found it difficult to believe that this young girl, with the long, brown hair and the look of pure innocence in the fine eyes, could be the faded, anxious, gossipy woman sitting here at her labor in this room.... She thought of the years before herself and of all the tragedy of womanhood.... There was silence between them for a space. Mrs. Brennan appeared as if she had been overpowered by some sad thought, for not a word fell from her as she began to untie the parcel of blouse material her customer had brought. There was no sound in the wide noontide stillness save the light fall of the album leaves as they were being turned.... Rebecca had paused again, and this time was studying the photos of two young men set in opposite pages. Both were arrayed in the fashions of 1890, and each had the same correct, stiff pose by an impossible-looking pedestal, upon which a French-gray globe reposed. But there was a great difference to be immediately observed as existing between the two men. One was handsome and of such a hearing as instantly appeals to feminine eyes. It was curious that they should have been placed in such contiguous contradistinction, for the other man seemed just the very opposite in every way to the one who was so handsome. It could not have been altogether by accident, was Rebecca's thought, and, with the intuition of a woman at work in her, she proceeded to lay the foundations of a romance.... Mrs. Brennan was observing her closely, and it grew upon her that she had been destined to bare her soul to this girl in this moment.

"That was the nice young man," said Rebecca, indicating the one who, despite his stiff pose by the pedestal, looked soldierly with his great mustache.

"Indeed he was all that," said Mrs. Brennan. "I met him when I was away off in England. He was a rich, grand young man, and as fond of me as the day was long; but he was a Protestant and fearful of his people to change his religion, and to be sure I could not change mine. For the sake of me holy religion I gave up all thoughts of him and married Ned Brennan, whose likeness you see on the other page."

Rebecca lifted her eyes from the album and looked full at Mrs. Brennan. She wondered how much truth could be in this story. The dressmaker was a coarse woman and not at all out of place in this mean room. She imagined the heavy husband of her choice as a suitable mate for her.

This sudden adoption of the attitude of a kind of martyr did not seem to fit well upon her. Rebecca could not so quickly imagine her as having done a noble and heroic thing for which she had not received sufficient beatification.

Rebecca was still turning the leaves. She had hurried through this little pageant of other generations, and was at the last pages. Now she was among people of the present, and her attention was no longer held by the peculiarities of the costumes.... Her mind was beginning to wander. Suddenly she was looking down upon a photo in the older style and the anachronism was startling. Had it been placed in any other portion of the album she might not have so particularly noticed it. It was the likeness of a dark, handsome man on horseback.

"Who was he?" she said, almost unconsciously.

A flush passed over the face of Mrs. Brennan, but she recovered herself by an effort. She smiled queerly through her confusion and said:

"Indeed 'tis you who ought to know that."

"How should I know?"—Rebecca was amazed.

"Don't you know Ulick Shannon?"

It was now Rebecca's turn to be confused.

Fancy this woman knowing that she had been talking just once with Ulick Shannon.... Evidently the tongue of this place had already begun to curl around her.

"But this is not Ulick Shannon!" She blushed as she found herself speaking his name.

"No, but it is the photo of his dead father, Henry Shannon."

Mrs. Brennan heaved a great sigh as she said this. She rose from her seat by the machine and moved towards the place where Rebecca was bending over the album. She gazed down at the picture of the dead man with moist eyes.... There was silence between them now for what seemed a long time. Rebecca became alarmed as she thought that she might have overstayed the half hour. At the school the priest or the inspector might have called and found her absent from her post.

She broke in abruptly upon Mrs. Brennan's fit of introspection, and gave a few hurried orders about the blouses.

"Will you be giving me the making of your next new costume?" said Mrs. Brennan.

"Well, I'm sorry—I don't think so. You see I have it being made already in Dublin."

"In Dublin itself? Well, well! that'll be the great style."

She felt it as an affront to her reputation that any one who lived in the neighborhood should patronize other places for their needs. She took such doings as exhibitions of spite and malice against her. And, somehow, she could not get rid of the idea now, although this girl evidently knew nothing of her history.

She was seeing Rebecca to the door when John Brennan came up the little path. She introduced him, and told how he was her son and, with vanity in her tones, that he was going to be a priest.

"That'll give her something to think of, with her slighting me be telling how she was having her costume made be another. A woman that's going to have a son a priest ought to be good enough to make for her, and she a whipster that's after coming from God knows where."

The mind of Mrs. Brennan was saying this to itself as she stood there at her own door gazing in pride upon her son. Rebecca Kerr was looking up into his face with a laugh in her eyes. He was such a nice young fellow, she was thinking. John Brennan was blushing in the presence of this girl and glancing shyly at her hair.

Suddenly she broke away from them with a laughing word upon her lips, ran out to the road, and down towards the school.

"She's a very nice girl, mother."

"Oh! indeed she's not much, John; and I knew well I wouldn't like her from the very first I heard tell of her coming."

CHAPTER XIII

Large posters everywhere announced the holding of a concert in Garradrimna. As in many other aspects of life in the village, it was not given to John Brennan to see their full meaning. He had not even seen in Thomas James, who posted the bills, a symbolic figure, but only one whom disaster had overtaken through the pursuit of his passion. For many a year had Thomas James gone about in this way, foretelling some small event in the life of Garradrimna. Now it was a race-meeting or a circus, again an auction or a fair. All the while he had been slipping into his present condition, and herein lay the curious pathos of him. For he would never post like this the passing of his own life; he would never set up a poster of Eternity.

It was curious to think of that, no poster at all of the exact moment amid the mass of Time when the Great White Angel would blow his blast upon the Shining Trumpet to awaken all Earth by its clear, wide ringing across the Seven Seas.

John Brennan spoke to his mother of the concert.

"The cheek of them I do declare, with their concert. People don't find it hard enough to get their money without giving it to them. Bits of shop-boys and shop-girls! But I suppose they want new clothes and costumes for the summer. I'll go bail you'll see them girls with new hats after this venture."

"The bills announce that it is for the Temperance Club funds."

"And them's the quare funds, you might say, and the quare club. Young fellows and young girls meeting in the one room to get up plays. No good can come of it."

"Of course we need not attend if we don't like."

"Ah, we must go all the same. If we didn't, 'tis what they would say mebbe that we hadn't the means, and so we must let them know that we have. It wouldn't be nice to see you away from it."

"I have no desire to go, mother, I assure you. A quiet evening more or less will not matter."

"But sure it'll be a bit of diversion and amusement."

"Yes, that is exactly what I was thinking, so I didn't see anything very wrong in going or in supporting those who organized it. But if you don't care to go, it does not matter."

"Ah, but wouldn't it be the quare thing to see your mother ignorant and not having a word to say about what was after passing to any one that would come in, and they knowing the whole thing? Now what you'll do for me, John, is this. You'll go into Phillips's this evening and get two of the most expensive tickets, one for yourself and one for me."

John Brennan had a momentary realization of the pitiful vanity behind this speech. He remained thinking while she went upstairs for the price of the tickets, for that must be her object, he fancied, in ascending into the upper story. He could hear her moving a trunk and opening it. The sounds came to him with perfect clearness in the still room and struck him with a sense of their little mournfulness, even though he was quite unaware that his mother had secretly begun the destruction of a bright portion of her life's dream.

In the evening he went to the village for the tickets.

"It'll be a grand turn-out," said Jimmy Phillips, as he took in the money and blinked in anticipation with his one eye.

"I'm sure," said John, as he left the little shop where you might buy the daily newspaper and sweets and everything.

He strolled up the street towards the old castle of the De Lacys. The local paper, published at Mullaghowen, was never tired of setting down its fame. The uncouth historians of the village had almost exhausted their adjectives in relating the exploits of this marauding baron of the Normans who had here built him a fortress, from which his companies of conquering freebooters had sallied forth so long ago. Yet, as an extraordinary mistake on the part of those who concerned themselves so intimately with the life around them, they had altogether missed the human side of the crumbling ruin. Of what romances of knighthood it had once been the scene? Of what visions of delight when fair women had met cuirassed gallants? Of all that pride which must have reared itself aloft in this place which was now the resort, by night, of the most humble creatures of the wild? Not one of them had ever been able to fancy the thoughts which must have filled the mind of Hugh De Lacy as he drew near this noble monument of his glory after some successful expedition against the chieftains of the Pale.

Through the thin curtain of the twilight John Brennan saw two figures stealing from the labyrinthine ways which led beneath the castle into what were known as "The Cells." These were dark, narrow places in which two together would be in close proximity, and it was out from them that this man and this woman were now stealing. He could not be certain of their identity, but they looked like two whom he knew.... And he had heard that Rebecca Kerr was going to sing at the concert, and also that Ulick Shannon was coaching the Garradrimna Dramatic Class in the play they were to produce, which was one he had seen at the Abbey Theater.... A curious thrill ran through him which was like a spasm of pain. Could it be this girl and this young man who had spoken with such disgusting intimacy of the female sex in the bar of the "North Leinster Arms" in Ballinamult ...? They went by a back way into the Club, where the rehearsals were now going forward.

John Brennan was sitting stiffly beside his mother in the front seats. Around and about him were people of renowned respectability, who had also paid two shillings each for their tickets. The seven publicans of Garradrimna were there, some with their wives, some with their wives and daughters, and some with their wives and daughters and sisters-in-law. The Clerk of the Union continually adjusting and re-adjusting his lemon-colored gloves. The old bespectacled maid from the Post Office sitting near the gray, bullet-headed postmaster, whose apoplectic jowl was shining. They were keeping up a continual chatter and buzz and giggle before the rise of the curtain. The jaws of the ancient postmistress never ceased to work, and those hot words of criticism and scorn which did not sizzle outwardly from her lips dropped inwardly to feed the fire of her mind, which was a volcano in perpetual eruption.

Mrs. Brennan sat in silence by the side of her son, in the pride of his presence, glad that he and she were here. She was as fine as any of them, for she kept fine raiment for such occasions. In the first place as an advertisement for her craft of dressmaker, and, secondly, to afford a cloak for her past, even as those among whom she sat cloaked their pasts in heavy garments of pride. Her attention was concentrated not so much upon the performance she was about to witness as upon the audience assembled to witness it. To her the audience was the concert, and, although she was speaking no word, she was as nervously observant as the old postmistress. She was concerned by the task before her, for would she not be in honor bound to "go over" all that passed to any one who might happen into the sewing-room next day, and lay everything bare with a searching and deadly analysis for her son John? Thus was she not distracted by the chattering and giggling, but perfectly at ease while her mind worked nimbly within the limits of its purpose.

The mind of John Brennan was not enjoying the same contentment. He was a little excited by the presence of Rebecca Kerr on a seat adjacent. She had a place on the program, and was awaiting her time to appear. His eye was dwelling upon her hair, which lifted gracefully from her white neck in a smooth wave of gold. It was the fairest thing in this clouded place of human fumes, and the dear softness from which it sprang such a recess of beauty.

The concert had at last begun. Harry Holton, the comic, was holding the stage and the audience was in convulsions. Harry Holton was a distant disciple of Harry Lauder. Having heard the funny Scotchman upon the gramophone he rather fancied that it was he who should have been Harry Lauder. In course of time, he had grown to think that it was Lauder and not himself who was doing the impersonation. His effort to be broadly Scotch, while the marks of the son of Erin were so strong upon him, was where, all unseen, his power to move towards laughter really lay. Yet the audience rocked its sides in crude mirth at this crude exhibition, and each man asked his neighbor was it not the funniest damned thing? The seven sleek publicans of Garradrimna threatened to explode.... John Brennan saw big beads of perspiration rise upon the comedian's brow and gleam in the sickly glare of the lamplight. Beyond the excitement, from behind the scenes, came a new sound—the popping of a cork—and through a chink in the back cloth he saw Ulick Shannon take his drink from the bottle.... Had Rebecca Kerr seen that as well as he or———. But his speculation was cut short by the exit of the comedian after many encores, amidst tumultuous applause.

Next came Agnes McKeon, a near relation of Monica's and the schoolmistress of Ballinamult. Her big spectacles gave her the look of her profession, and although she sang well in a pleasing contralto, she appeared stiff and unalluring in her white dress, which was starched to a too strong resplendence. John heard two old maids with scraggy necks remarking, not upon the power of Miss McKeon's voice, but upon the extraordinary whiteness of her dress, and saying it was grand surely, but they anxiously wondered were all her garments as clean for they were ready to credit her with extreme slovenliness of habit.

The play was the notable event of the evening. Although the work of a famous Abbey playwright, it had been evidently re-written for Harry Holton, who was the principal character. It was purely a Harry Holton show. Dramatic point and sequence were sacrificed to give scope to his renowned abilities. The other players would seem to have merged themselves to give him prominence. But the ladies had not merged their natural vanity. One in particular, who was supposed to represent an old woman of Ireland, wore an attractive dress which was in the prevailing fashion. It was the illiterate pronunciation of even the simplest words which chiefly amused John Brennan. Herein might be detected the touch of Ulick Shannon, who, in coaching the production, had evidently added this means of diversion for his own amusement. John fancied that his friend must be enjoying it hugely in there behind the scenes.

When the play had been concluded by Harry Holton giving a few steps of a dance, John Brennan saw Rebecca moving towards the stage. He observed the light grace with which she went to the ordeal. Here was no self-consciousness, but instead that easy quietness which is a part of dignity.... It was Ulick Shannon who held aside the curtain allowing her to pass in upon the stage.

"Well now, isn't that one the brazen thing?"

This was the expression of opinion which came clearly from out the whispering and giggling. It was an unpardonable offense to appear in public like this without a certain obvious fluttering and fear which it was one of Garradrimna's most notable powers to create. It was a great flout. Even his mother was moved to nudge him, so unusual was the method of this strange girl, appearing in public before the place into which she had come to earn a living.

But she was singing. Rebecca Kerr was singing, and to John Brennan this was all he wished to know. He trembled as he listened and grew weary with delight. He became nervous, as before some unaccountable apprehension, and turned to his mother. She was looking quizzically at the girl on the stage. But the stage to him was now a sort of haze through which there moved ever little dancing specks.

The concert was over and his mind had not yet returned to realization. Rebecca had not come from behind the scenes. He moved with his mother out into the night, and, as they went, glanced around the corner of the hall. He saw Rebecca Kerr and Ulick Shannon standing within the shadow of the surrounding wood. He spoke no word to his mother as they went down the road towards the house in the valley.

CHAPTER XIV

As if from the excitement of the concert, John Brennan felt weary next morning. He had been awake since early hours listening to the singing of the birds in all the trees near the house. The jolly sounds came to him as a great comfort. Consequently it was with an acute sensation of annoyance that there crowded in upon his sense of hearing little distracting noises. Now it was the heavy rumble of a cart, again the screech of a bicycle ridden by Farrell McGuinness on his way to Garradrimna for the letters of his rounds; and, continually, the hard rasp of nailed boots upon the gravel of the road.

His mother was moving about in the sewing-room beneath. He could hear the noise made by her scissors as, from time to time, she laid it down and picked it up again, while, mingled with these actions, occasionally came up to him the little, unmusical song of the machine. His father was still snoring.

Last night Rebecca Kerr had shone in his eyes.... But how exactly had she appeared before the eyes of Garradrimna and the valley? After what manner would she survive the strong blast of talk? The outlook of his mother would be representative of the feeling which had been created. Yet he felt that it would be repugnant to him to speak with his mother of Rebecca Kerr. There would be that faded woman, looking at him with a kind of loving anxiety which seemed always to have the effect of crushing him back relentlessly towards the realities of the valley and his own reality. After his thoughts of last night and this morning he hated to face his mother.

When at last he went down into the room where she sat sewing he had such an unusual look in his eyes as seemed to require the solace of an incident to fill it. If he had expected to find a corresponding look upon his mother's face he was disappointed. It seemed to wear still the quizzical expression of last night, and a slight curl at the corners of her mouth told that her mind was being sped by some humorous or satirical impulse.

"Whatever was the matter with you last night, John?" she asked.

She did not give him time to frame an answer, but went on:

"And I dying down dead to talk to you about the concert, I could not get you to speak one word to me and we coming home."

He noticed that she was in good heart, and, although it was customary with him to be pleased to see his mother in a mood of gladness, he could not enter into laughter and gossip with her now.

But she could not be silent. This small expedition into the outer world of passing events was now causing her mind to leap, with surprising agility, from topic to topic.... Yet what was striking John more than her talk, and with a more arresting realization, was, that although the hour of his Mass-going was imminent, she was not reminding him or urging him to remembrance of the good custom.... At last he was driven by some scruple to remind her of the time, and it was her answer that finally amazed him:

"Ah, sure you mightn't go to-day, John. You're tired and all to that, I know, and I want to tell you.... He! he! he! Now wasn't it the funniest thing to see the schoolmistress of Ballinamult and the schoolmistress of Tullahanogue and they up upon the one stage with Harry Holton's dramatics making sport for a lot of grinning idiots? Like a couple of circus girls they were, the brazen things! Indeed Miss Kerr is the bold-looking hussy, with not a bit of shame in her at all. But sure we may say she fell among her equals, for there wasn't much class connected with it anyhow."

"I think Ulick Shannon was knocking about the stage."

The words strayed, without much sense of meaning or direction, out of the current of his musing, but they produced a swift and certain effect upon Mrs. Brennan. Her eyes seemed to cloud suddenly behind her glasses.

"Aye ... I wonder who was the girl he went off with through the wood as we came out. Never fear it was the new schoolmistress."

She said this with a curious, dead quietness in her tones, and when she had spoken she seemed instantly sorry that the words had slipped from her lips.... It seemed a queer thing to say to her son and he going on to be a priest.

John thought it very strange that she too should have observed this incident, which he had imagined must have been hidden from all eyes save his own. He now wondered how many more must have seen it as he tried to recall the sensations with which it had filled him.... But beyond this remarkable endeavor of his mind his mother was again speaking:

"If you went now, you'd be in time for half-past eight Mass."

He did not fail to notice the immediate change which had taken place in her, and wondered momentarily what could have been its sudden cause. He was beginning to notice of late that she had grown more and more subject to such unaccountable fits.

In his desire to obey her he was still strong, but, this morning, as he walked along to Garradrimna he was possessed by a certain feeling of annoyance which seemed to strain the bond that stretched between them.

In the chapel he knelt beside Charlie Clarke, like the voteens around them, with a lifeless acquiescence in the ceremony. He was here not because his heart was here, but merely because his mother had wished it. When his lips moved, in mechanical mimicry of the priest, he felt that the way of the hypocrite must be hard and lonely.

When he came out, upon the road he was confused to find himself face to face with Rebecca Kerr. It seemed a trick of coincidence that he should meet her now, for it had never happened on any other morning. Then he suddenly remembered how his mother had kept him late from "eight o'clock" by her talk of the concert, and it was now Miss Kerr's school-going time.... She smiled and spoke to him.

She looked handsome as she moved there along the road from the house of Sergeant McGoldrick to the Girls' School of Tullahanogue. She was in harmony with the beauty of the morning. There had been a dull pain upon his mind since he had last seen her, but already it was gone.

Although the concert might appear as the immediate subject to which their minds would turn, this was not so. They began to talk of places and things away from Garradrimna.

She spun for his amusement many little yarns of the nuns who conducted the college where she had been trained. He told her stories of the priests who taught in the English college where he was being educated for the priesthood. They enlarged upon the peculiarities of monastic establishments.

"And you're going to be a priest?" she said, looking up into his face suddenly with dancing eyes.

Such a question had never before been put to him in exactly this way.

"I am.... At least, I think so.... Oh, yes!" he faltered.

She laughed in a ringing, musical way that seemed to hold just the faintest trace of mockery in its tones, but it seemed, next instant, to be only by way of preface to another conventual tale which she proceeded to tell.

Through the period of this story they did not notice that they were being stared at by those they were meeting upon the road.... As she chatted and laughed, his eyes would be straying, in spite of him, to that soft place upon her neck from which her hair sprang upward.

It was with painful abruptness that she said: "Good morning, Mr. Brennan!" and went into the old, barrack-like school.

CHAPTER XV

When John regained the house he saw that his father's boots had disappeared from their accustomed place beside the fire. No doubt he had gone away in them to Garradrimna. He had not met him on the road, but there was a short way across the fields and through the woods, a backward approach to three of the seven publichouses along which Ned Brennan, some rusty plumber's tool in his hand and his head downcast, might be seen passing on any day.

He did not go straight into the sewing-room, for the door was closed and he could hear the low murmur of talk within. It must be some customer come to his mother, he thought, or else some one who had called in off the road to talk about the concert. Immediately he realized that he was wrong in both surmises, for it was the voice of Marse Prendergast raised in one of its renowned outbursts of supplication.

"Now I suppose it's what you think that you're the quare, clever woman, Nan Byrne, with your refusing me continually of me little needs; but you'd never know what I'd be telling on you some day, and mebbe to your grand son John."

"Sssh—sssh—sure I'll get it for you when he goes from the kitchen."

This last was in a low tone and spoken by his mother.

"Mebbe it's what you're ashamed to let him see you giving to me. That's a grand thing now, and I knowing what I know!"

"Can't you be easy now and maybe 'tis a whole shilling I'll be giving you in a few minutes."

This was altogether too generous of his mother. It gave scope to Marse Prendergast to exercise her tyranny. Her threat was part of the begging convention she had framed for herself, and so it did not move him towards speculation or suspicion. His mind drifted on to the enjoyment of other thoughts, the girl he had just walked with down the valley, the remembered freshness of the morning road. He came out to the door. The little kitchen garden stretched away from his feet. An abandoned spade stood up lonely and erect in the middle of the cabbage-plot. Around it were a few square feet of freshly-turned earth. It was the solitary trace of his existence that his father had left behind.... As the mind of John Brennan came to dwell upon the lonely spectacle of the spade the need for physical exertion grew upon him.

He went out into the little garden and lifted the rude implement of cultivation in his hand. He had not driven it many times into the soft clay of the cabbage-bed when a touch of peace seemed to fall upon him. The heavy burden that had occupied his mind was falling into the little trench that was being made by the spade.

He had become so interested in his task that he had not heard his mother go upstairs nor seen Marse Prendergast emerge from the house some moments later.

The old shuiler called out to him in her high, shrill voice:

"That's right, John! That's right! 'Tis glad myself is to see you doing something useful at last. Digging the cabbage-plot, me sweet gosoon, and your father in Garradrimna be this time with his pint in his hand!"

Mrs. Brennan had followed her to the door, and her cruelty was stirred to give the sore cut by reviving the old dread.

"That's the lad! That's the lad! But mind you don't dig too far, for you could never tell what you'd find. And indeed it would be the quare find you might say!"

He laughed as she said this, for he remembered that, as a child she had entertained him with the strangest stories of leprecauns and their crocks of gold, which were hidden in every field. The old woman passed out on the road, and his mother came over to him with a pitiful look of sadness in her eyes.

"Now, John, I'm surprised at you to have a spade in your hand before Marse Prendergast and all. That's your father's work and not yours, and you with your grand education."

The speech struck him as being rather painful to hear, and he felt as if he should like to say: "Well, what is good enough for my father ought to be good enough for me!" But this, to his mother, might have looked like a back-answer, a piece of impertinence, so he merely stammered in confusion: "Oh, sure I was only exercising and amusing myself. When this little bit is finished I'm going down to have a read by the lake."

"That's right, John!" she said in a flat, sad voice, and turned back to her endless labor.

He stopped, his hands folded on the handle-end of the spade, and fell into a condition of dulness which even the slightest labor of the body brings to those unaccustomed to it. All things grew so still of a sudden. There seemed to come a perfect lull in the throbbing, nervous realization of his brain from moment to moment.... He felt himself listening for the hum of his mother's machine, but it was another sound that came to him—the desolating sound of her lonely sobbing. She was crying to herself there now in the sewing-room and mourning forever as if for some lost thing.... There were her regular sobs, heavy with an eternal sadness as he listened to them. Into such acute self-consciousness had his mood now moved that he could not imagine her crying as being connected with anything beyond himself. He was the perpetual cause of all her pain.... If only she would allow him, for short spaces, to go out of her mind they might both come into the enjoyment of a certain freedom, but sometimes the most trivial incident seemed to put her out so. This morning she had been in such heart and humor, and last night so interested in the concert, and here now she was in tears. It could not have been the visit of Marse Prendergast or her talk, for there was nobody so foolish, he thought, as to take any notice of either. It must have been the digging and the fact that people passing the road might see him. Now was not that foolish of her, for did not Father O'Keeffe himself dig in his own garden with his own two blessed hands ...? But he must bend in obedience to her desire, and go walking like a leisured gentleman through the valley. He was looking forward to this with dread, for, inevitably, it must throw him back upon his own thoughts.

As he came down past the school he could hear a dull drone from among the trees. The school had not yet settled down to the business of the day, and the scholars were busy with the preparation of their lessons. John stopped by the low wall, which separated its poor playground from the road, to gaze across at the hive of intellect. Curious that his mother should now possess a high contempt for this rude academy where he had been introduced to learning. But he had not yet parted company with his boyhood. He was remembering the companions of his schooldays and how this morning preparation had been such a torture. Still moving about the yard before his formal entrance to the school, was Master Donnellan. As John Brennan saw him now he appeared as one misunderstood by the people of the valley, and yet as one in whom the lamp of the intellect was set bright and high. But beyond this immediate thought of him he appeared as a man with overthrown ambitions and shattered dreams, whose occasional outbursts of temper for these reasons had often the effect of putting him at enmity with the parents of the children.

Master Donnellan was a very slave of the ferrule. He had spent his brains in vain attempts to impart some knowledge to successive generations of dunces of the fields. It had been his ambition to be the means of producing some great man whose achievements in the world might be his monument of pride. But no pupil of his in the valley school had ever arisen as a great man. Many a time, in the long summer evenings, when the day would find it hard to disappear from Ireland, he would come quietly to the old school with a step of reverence, and going into the moldy closet, where all the old roll-books and register-books were kept, take them down one by one and go searching through the lists of names. His mind would be filled with the ringing achievements of men who had become notable in the world.... Not a trace of any of those famous names could he find here, however far he might search in all the musty books until the day had faded.... Then he would rely upon his memory in a further aspect of his search. He had not even produced a local great man. In his time no priests had come out of the valley. There was a strange thing now—no priests, and it was a thing that was always said by angry mothers and fathers when they called at the valley school to attack him for his conduct towards their children—"And you never to have made a priest or a ha'porth!" It was not the unreasonableness of their words that annoyed him, but rather the sense of impotence with which they filled him.... If only it would happen that he could say he had produced one famous man. A priest would be sufficiently fine to justify him in the eyes of the valley. It was so strange that, although he had seen many young men move towards high attainment, some fatality had always happened to avert his poor triumph. He thought of young Brennan as his present hope and pride.

John went on towards the lake. When he came to the water's edge he was filled with a sense of peace. He sat down beneath one of the fir trees and, in the idleness of his mood, began to pick up some of the old dried fir-cones which were fallen beneath. They appeared to him as things peculiarly bereft of any sap or life. He gathered until he had a handful and then cast them from him one by one on the surface of the water. It seemed a surprising thing that the small eddies which the light splashes of them made rolled distantly to the shores of the little lake. He began to wonder would his life come to be like that—a small thing to be flung by the Hand of Fate and creating its little ripple to eddy to the far shores of Time.

"Me sound man, John!"

It was the voice of Shamesy Golliher coming from behind a screen of reeds where he had been fishing.

"'Tis a warm day," he said, pushing back his faded straw hat from his brow, "Glory be to the Son of God!"

This was a pious exclamation, but the manner of its intonation seemed to make it comical for John Brennan laughed and Shamesy Golliher laughed.

"Now isn't them the clever, infernal little gets of fishes? The divil a one can I catch only the size of pinkeens, and I wanting to go to Garradrimna with a hell of a thirst!"

"And is that all you have troubling you?" said John.

"Is that all? Begad if it isn't enough after last night. If the priests knew all the drink that bees drunk at concerts in aid of Temperance Halls you wouldn't see a building of that kind in the country.

"Now down with me last night to the concert with me two lovely half-pints of malt. Well, to make a long story short, I finished one of them before I went in. I wasn't long inside, and I think it was while Harry Holton was singing, when who should give me a nudge only Hubert Manning: 'Are ye coming out, Shamesy?' says he. He had two bottles of stout and a naggin, and we had them finished before Harry Holton had done his first song. I was striving for to crush back into me place when who should I knock against only Farrell McGuinness? He had a lot of bottles in his pocket. He seemed to have about four dozen of stout on his person, according to the noise he made: 'For the honor of Jases,' says he, 'will you not spill me porter?' But then when he saw it was me he had in it: 'Come to hell oura this,' says he, 'into the night air.' I was so glad to see that he hadn't broken his bottles, I introduced th'other half pint. Sure he nearly swallowed it, bottle and all. Then we fell to at the porter, and such a bloody piece of drinking never was seen. And it wasn't that we had plenty of drink of our own, but strange people were coming running through the wood putting half-pints and naggins into our mouths just as if we were little sucking childer. I fell a corpse under a tree about eleven. I don't know how long I was insensible, but when I came to I had a quare feeling that I was in Hell or some place. I wasn't able to move an inch, I was that stiff and sick.... Somewhere near me I could hear two whispering and hugging in the darkness. They were as close as ever they could be. I couldn't stir to get a better look for fear they'd hear me. But there was quare goings on I can tell you, things I wouldn't like to mention or describe. Whisper, I'm near sure it was Ulick Shannon and the schoolmistress, Miss Kerr, or whatever the hell her name is———."

Shamesy's sickening realism was brought to an abrupt end by the ducking of his cork, which had been floating upon the surface of the water. There was a short moment of joyous excitement and then a dying perch lay on the grass by the side of John Brennan.

He viewed with sorrow that clean, shining thing wriggling there beneath the high heavens. Its end had come through the same pitiful certainty as that of the rabbits which had aforetime contributed to the thirst of Shamesy, who presently said with delight:

"Now I have the correct number. I can sell them for sixpence in 'The World's End,' and you'd never know the amount of good drink that sixpence might bring."

He prepared to take his departure, but ere he went across the hill he turned to John and said:

"That was the fine walk you were doing with Ulick Shannon's girl this morning! She was in great form after last night."

He said it with such a leer of suggestion as cast John, still blushing, back into his gloom.

CHAPTER XVI

Last night and this morning, what Shamesy Golliher had told him of last night and said of the walk with Rebecca this morning—all this was now recurring clearly to his mind, although Shamesy had long since disappeared across the sweep of the hill on his way to Garradrimna.

Mrs. Brennan had so recently reminded her son of his coming exaltation that the suggestion was now compelling him beyond the battle of his thought to picture himself as a priest ordained. Yet an immense gulf of difference still separated him from the condition of Father O'Keeffe, for instance. His thought had been further helped to move this way by the sudden appearance of Father O'Keeffe riding along The Road of the Dead.

John did not see the man as he really was. Yet it was the full reality of him that was exercising a subconscious influence upon his mind and helping, with other things, to turn his heart away from the priesthood.

Father O'Keeffe came directly from that class so important in Ireland—the division of the farmer class which has come to be known as "The Grabbers." The word "grabber" had not been invented to describe a new class, but rather to denote the remarkable character of a class already in existence. That was their innermost nature, these farmers, to be close-fisted and to guard with an almost savage tenacity those possessions to which they had already attained. It was notable also that they were not too careful or particular as to the means they employed to come into possession. This was the full answer to the question why so many of them put a son on for the Church. It was a double reason, to afford a means of acquiring still further and to be as an atonement in the sight of Heaven for the means they had used in acquiring thus far. This at once appeared amazingly true if one applied it to the case of Father O'Keeffe, who could on occasion put on such a look of remoteness from this world, that it was difficult to set about analyzing him by any earthly standard. Yet, among all the *pedigrees* she had read for him, as a notable example in Mrs. Brennan's crowd of examples, had continually appeared and re-appeared this family of O'Keeffe. His mother had always endeavored to fix firmly in his mind the wonder of their uprise. It was through the gates of the Church that the O'Keeffes had gone to their enjoyment. No doubt they had denied themselves to educate this Louis O'Keeffe who had become P.P. of Garradrimna, but their return had been more than satisfying. There was now no relation of his to the most distant degree of blood who did not possess great comfort and security in the land.

At bottom Father O'Keeffe was still a man of the clay and loved the rich grass and the fine cattle it produced. He had cattle in every quarter of the parish. Men bought them and saw to their fattening and sold them for him, even going so far as adding the money to his account in the bank. He had most discreetly used a seeming unworldliness to screen his advance upon the ramparts of Mammon. Citing the examples of Scripture, he consorted with notable, though suddenly converted, sinners, and, when some critic from among the common people was moved to speak his mind as one of the converted sinners performed a particularly unscrupulous stroke of business, he was immediately silenced by the unassailable spectacle of his parish priest walking hand in hand with the man whose actions he was daring to question. The combination was of mutual benefit; the gombeen man, the auctioneer and the publican were enabled to proceed with their swindle of the poor by maintaining his boon companionship.

Thus, while publicly preaching the admonishing text of the camel and the rich man and the needle's eye, Father O'Keeffe was privately engaged in putting himself in such a condition that the task of negotiating the needle's eye might be as difficult to him as the camel. He went daily for a walk, reading his office, and returned anxiously scanning stock exchange quotations and letters from cattle salesmen in Dublin. But in spite of this he was a sportsman, and thought nothing of risking a ten-pound note upon a horse or a night's card-play.

When he first came to the parish his inclinations were quickly determined. In the whirl of other interests cards had fallen into disuse in Garradrimna. They had come to be considered old-fashioned, but now suddenly they became "all the rage." Old card-tables were rediscovered and renewed, and it was said that Tommy Williams was compelled to order several gross of playing cars— for, what the "elite" of the parish did, the "commonality" must needs follow and do. Thus was a public advantage of doubtful benefit created; for laboring men were known to lose their week's wages to the distress of their wives and children.... At the "gorgeous card-plays" never an eyelid was lifted when Father O'Keeffe "renayged."

These took place in the houses of shopkeepers and strong farmers, and were cultivated to a point of excessive brilliance. Ancient antagonists of the tongue met upon this new field, and strategic attempts were made to snatch Father O'Keeffe as a prize of battle. Thus was an extravagant sense of his value at once created and, as in all such cases, the worst qualities of the man came to be developed. His natural snobbishness, for one thing, which led him to associate a great deal with the gilded youth of Garradrimna—officials of the Union and people of that kind who had got their positions through every effort of bribery and corruption. At athletic sports or coursing matches you would see him among a group of them, while they smoked stinking "Egyptian" cigarettes up into his face.

Yet it must not be thought that Father O'Keeffe neglected the ladies. In evenings in the village he might be seen standing outside the worn drapery counters back-biting between grins and giggles with the women of the shops. This curious way of spending the time had once led an irreverent American to describe him as "the flirtatious shop-boy of Garradrimna."

His interest in the female sex often led him upon expeditions beyond the village. Many a time he might be seen riding his old, fat, white horse, so strangely named, "King Billy," down some rutted boreen on the way to a farmer's house where there were big daughters with weighty fortunes. Those were match-making expeditions when he had come to tell them of his brother Robert O'Keeffe and his broad acres.... While "King Billy" was comforting himself with a plentiful feed of oats, he would be sitting in the musty parlor with the girl and her mother, taking wine and smoking cigars, which were kept in every house since it had come to be known that Father O'Keeffe was fond of them. He generally smoked a good few at a sitting, and those he did not consume he carried away in his pocket for future use in his den at the Presbytery.

"Isn't Father O'Keeffe, God bless him, the walking terror for cigars?" was all the comment ever made upon this extraordinary habit.

Robert O'Keeffe, in the intentions of his brother, was a much-married man, for there was not a house in the parish holding a marriageable girl into which Father O'Keeffe had not gone to get him a match. He had enlarged upon the excellence of his brother, upon his manners and ways and the breadth of his fields.

"He's the grand, fine man, is Robert," he would say, by way of giving a final touch to the picture.

Upon those whose social standing was not a thing of any great certitude this had always a marked effect towards their own advantage and that of Father O'Keeffe. It gave them a certain pride in their own worth to have a priest calling attentively at the house and offering his brother in marriage. It would be a gorgeous thing to be married to a priest's brother, and have your brother-in-law with power in his hands to help you out of many a difficulty. He never inquired after the cattle their fathers were grazing free of charge for him until he would be leaving the house.

John Brennan followed the black figure upon the white horse down all The Road of the Dead until Father O'Keeffe had disappeared among the trees which surrounded the Schools of Tullahanogue, where he was making a call.

CHAPTER XVII

John now saw Ulick Shannon coming towards him across the Hill of Annus. It was strange that he should be appearing now whose presence had just been created by the Rabelaisian recital of Shamesy Golliher. As he came along boldly his eyes roamed cheerfully over the blue expanse of water and seemed to catch something there which moved him to joyous whistling. John Brennan felt a certain amount of reserve spring up between them as they shook hands.... For a moment that seemed to lengthen out interminably the two young men were silent. The lake was without a ripple in the intense calm of the summer day.... Suddenly it reflected the movement of them walking away, arm in arm, towards the village.

It was high noontide when they reached Garradrimna. The Angelus was ringing. Men had turned them from their various occupations to bend down for a space in prayer. The drunkards had put away the pints from their mouths in reverence. The seven sleek publicans were coming to their doors with their hats in their hands, beating their breasts in a frenzy of zeal and genuflecting. Yet, upon the appearance of the students, a different excitement leaped up to animate them. They began to hurry their prayers, the words becoming jumbled pell mell in their mouths as they cleared a way for their tongues to say to one another the thing they wanted to say of the two young men.

By their God, there was John Brennan and Ulick Shannon coming into Garradrimna in the middle of the day. To drink, they at once supposed. Their tongues had been finding fine exercise upon Ulick Shannon for a considerable time, but it was certainly a comfort to have the same to say of John Brennan. A clerical student coming up the street with a Dublin scamp. That was a grand how-d'ye-do! But sure they supposed, by their God again, that it was only what she deserved (they were referring to Mrs. Brennan).

Her mention at once brought recollection of her story, and it came to be discussed there in the heat of the day until the lonely woman, who was still crying probably as she sat working by her machine in the little house in the valley, became as a corpse while the vultures of Garradrimna circled round it flapping great wings in glee.

The students strode on, reciting the Angelus beneath their breaths with a devotion that did not presently give place to any worldly anxiety. They were doing many things now, as if they formed a new personality in which the will and the inclination of each were merged. They turned into McDermott's, and it seemed their collective intention from the direction they took upon entering the shop to take refuge in the retirement of the particular portion known as Connellan's office. It was the place where Mick Connellan, the local auctioneer, transacted business on Fridays. On all other days it was considered the more select and secluded portion of this publichouse. But when they entered it was occupied. Padna Padna, the ancient drunkard, was sitting by the empty grate poking the few drawn corks in it as if they were coals. He was speaking to himself in mournful jeremiads, and after the fashion of one upon whom a great sorrow has fallen down.

"Now what the hell does he want with his mission, and it too good we are? A mission, indeed, for to make us pay him money every night, and the cosht of everything, drink and everything. He, he, he! To pay the price of a drink every night to hear the missioners denounce drink. Now that's the quarest thing ever any one heard. To go pay the price of a drink for hearing a man that doesn't even know the taste of it say that drink is not good for the human soul. Begad Father O'Keeffe is the funny man!"

After this fashion did Padna Padna run on in soliloquy. He had seen many a mission come to bring, in the words of the good missioners, "a superabundance of grace to the parish," and seen it go without bringing any appreciable addition of grace to him or any change in his way of life. It seemed a pity that his tradition had set Padna Padna down as a Christian, and would not allow him to live his life upon Pagan lines and in peace. The struggle which continually held occupation of his mind was one between Christian principles and Pagan inclinations. He now began whispering to himself—"The Book of God! The Book of God! A fellow's name bees written in the Book of God!" ... So absorbed was he in his immense meditation that he had hardly noticed the entry of the students. But as he became aware of their presence he stumbled to his feet and gripping John Brennan by the arm whispered tensely: "Isn't that a fact, young fellow, that one's name bees down there always, and what one does, and that it's never blotted out?"

"It is thus we are told," said John, speaking dogmatically and as if he were repeating a line out of the Bible.

Padna Padna, as he heard these words and recognized the voice of their speaker, put on what was really his most gruesome expression. He stripped his shrunken gums in a ghastly little smile, and a queer "Tee-Hee!" issued from his furrowed throat.... Momentarily his concern for Eternity was forgotten in a more immediate urgency of this world. He gripped John still more tightly and in a higher whisper said: "Are ye able to stand?"

It was a strange anti-climax and at once betrayed his sudden descent in the character of his meditation, from thinking of what the Angel had written of him to his immortal longing for what had determined the character of that record regarding immortality.

"Yes, I'll stand," said Ulick, breaking in upon John Brennan's reply to Padna Padna and pushing the bell.

Mr. McDermott himself, half drunk and smelling of bad whiskey, came in and soon the drinks were before them. New life seemed to come pushing into the ancient man as he took his "half one." He looked up in blind thankfulness into their faces, his eyes running water and his mouth dribbling like that of a young child.... His inclinations were again becoming rapidly Pagan.... From smiling dumbly he began to screech with laughter, and moved from the room slowly tapping his way with his short stick.... He was going forth to fresh adventures. Spurred on by this slight addition of drink he would be encouraged to enter the other six publichouses of Garradrimna, and no man could tell upon what luck he might happen to fall. So fortunate might his half-dozen expeditions prove that he would probably return to the house of the good woman who was his guardian, led by Shamesy Golliher, or some other one he would strike up with in the last dark pub, as if he were a toddling infant babbling foolish nonsense about all the gay delights which had been his of old. The mad drives from distant villages upon his outside car, his passengers in the same condition as himself—a state of the wildest abandon, and dwelling exultingly in that moment wherein they might make fitting models for a picture by Jack B. Yeats.

Ulick and John were now alone. The day outside was hot and still upon the dusty street, but this office of Connellan's was a cool place like some old cellar full of forgotten summers half asleep in wine.... They were entering still deeper into the mood of one another.... Ulick had closed the door when Padna Padna had passed through, tapping blindly as he moved towards the far places of the village. He would seem to have gone for no other purpose than to publish broadcast the presence of Ulick Shannon and John Brennan together in McDermott's, and they drinking. For now the door of Connellan's office was being opened and closed every few minutes. People were calling upon the pretense of looking for other people, and going away leaving the door open wide behind them so that some others might come also and see for themselves the wonderful thing that was happening.... Padna Padna was having such a time as compared favorably with the high times of old. A "half-one" of malt from every man he brought to see the sight was by no means a small reward. And so he was coming and going past the door like a sentry on guard of some great treasure which increased in value from moment to moment. He was blowing upon his fingers and tapping his lips and giggling and screeching with merriment down in his shivering frame.

And most wonderful of all, the two young men who were creating all this excitement were quite unconscious of it.... They were talking a great deal, but each, as it were, from behind the barricade of his personality, for each was now beginning for the first time to notice a peculiar thing. They were discovering that their personalities were complementary. John lacked the gift, which was Ulick's, of stating things brilliantly out of life and experience and the views of those modern authors whom he admired. On the other hand, he seemed to possess a deeper sense of the relative realities of certain things, a faculty which sprang out of his ecclesiastical training and which held no meaning for Ulick, who spoke mockingly of such things. Ulick skimmed lightly over the surface of life in discussing it; John was inclined to plow deeply.

Suddenly a desire fell upon John to hear Ulick discuss again those matters he had talked of at the "North Leinster Arms" in Ballinamult. It was very curious that this should be the nature of his thoughts now, this inclination towards things which from him should always have remained far distant and unknown.... But it may have been that some subtle impulse had stirred in him, and that he now wished to see whether the outlook of Ulick had changed in any way through his rumored friendship with Rebecca Kerr. Would it be a cleaner thing and purified through power of that girl? He fondly fancied that no thought at all could be soiled within the splendid precinct of her presence.

Josie Guinan, the new barmaid of McDermott's, came in to attend them with other and other drinks. Her bosom was attractive and ample, although her hair was still down upon her back in rich brown plaits.... She dallied languorously within the presence of the two young men.... Ulick began to tell some of the stories he had told to Mary Essie, and she stood even as brazenly enjoying them with her back to the door closed behind her. Then the two came together and whispered something, and a vulgar giggle sprang up between them.

And to think that this was the man to whom Rebecca Kerr might be giving the love of her heart.... If John had seen as much of life as the other he would have known that Ulick was the very kind of man who, at all times, has most strongly appealed to women. Yet it was in this moment and in this place that he fell in love with Rebecca.... He became possessed of an infinite willingness to serve and protect her, and it was upon the strength of his desire that he arose.

Through all this secret, noble passage, Ulick remained laughing as at some great joke. He, too, was coming into possession of a new joy, for he was beginning to glimpse the conflagration of another's soul. Out of sheer devilment, and in conspiracy with Josie Guinan, he had caused John Brennan's drink, the small, mild measure of port wine, to be dosed with flaming whiskey. Even the wine in the frequency of its repetition had already been getting the better of him. They had been hours sitting here, and outside the day was fading.

John began to stutter now in the impotence of degradation which was upon him. His thoughts were all burning into one blazing thought. The small room seemed suddenly to cramp and confine his spirit as if it were a prison cell.... And Ulick was still smiling that queer smile of his with his thick red lips and sunken eyes.

He sprang towards the door and, turning the handle, rushed out into the air.... Soon he was fleeing as if from some Unknown Force, staggering between the rows of the elms which stretched all along the road into the valley. It had rained a shower and the strong, young leaves held each its burden of pearly drops. A light wind now stirred them and like an aspergillus they flung a blessing down upon him as he passed. And ever did he mutter her name to himself as he stumbled on:

"Rebecca Kerr, Rebecca Kerr, I love you, Rebecca, I love you surely! Oh, my dear Rebecca!"

She was moving before him, with her hair all shining through the twilight.

"Oh, dear Rebecca! I love you! Oh, my dear!"

He turned The Road of the Dead and down by the lake, where he lay in the quiet spot from which Ulick Shannon had taken him away to Garradrimna. There he remained until far on in the evening, when his mother, concerned for his welfare, came to look for him. She found him sleeping by the lake.

She had no notion of how he had passed the evening. Her imagination was, after all, only a very small thing and worked rigorously within the romantic confines of the holy stories which were her continual reading. When she had awakened him she asked a characteristic question:

"And I suppose, John, you're after seeing visions and things have appeared to you?"

"Yes, mother, I have seen a vision, I think," he said, as he opened his eyes and blinked stupidly at the lake. He was still midway between two conditions, but he was not noticeable to her, who could not have imagined the like.

These were the only words he spoke to her before he went to bed.

Back in McDermott's a great crowd thronged the public bar. Every man seemed to be in high glee and a hum of jubilation hung low between them. A momentous thing had happened, and it was of this great event they were talking. *John Brennan had left the house and he was reeling.* Men from the valley foregathered in one group and, as each new-comer arrived, the news was re-broken. It was about the best thing that had ever happened. The sudden enrichment of any of their number could not have been half so welcome in its importance.

Padna Padna and Shamesy Golliher were standing in one corner taking sup for sup.

"Damn it, but it was one of the greatest days ever I seen in Garradrimna since the ould times. It was a pity you missed of it," said Padna Padna. "If you were to see him!"

"Sure I'm after seeing him, don't I tell ye, lying a corpse be the lake."

"A corpse be the lake. He, he, he! Boys-a-day! Boys-a-day!"

CHAPTER XVIII

Mrs. Brennan, although she pondered it deeply, had made no advance towards full realization of her son's condition by the lakeside. Yet John felt strangely diffident about appearing before her next morning. It seemed to him that another attack had been made upon the bond between them. But when at last he came into the sewing-room she was smiling, although there was a sinking feeling around his heart as he looked upon her. Yet this would pass, he hoped, when they began to talk.

The children were going the road to school, and it was the nature of Mrs. Brennan that she must needs be making comment upon what was passing before her eyes.

"God help the poor, little girls," she cried, "sure 'tis the grand example they're being set by that new one, Miss Kerr, with her quare dresses and her light ways. They say she was out half the night after the concert with Ulick Shannon, and that Mrs. McGoldrick and the Sergeant are in terror of their lives for fear of robbers or the likes, seeing that they have to leave the door on the latch for her to come in at any time she pleases from her night-walking. And the lad she bees with that's after knocking about Dublin and couldn't be good anyway. But sure, be the same token, there's a touch of Dublin about her too. How well she wouldn't give me the making of her new dress? But I suppose I'm old-fashioned in my cut. Old-fashioned, how are ye; and I buying *Weldon's Ladies' Journal* every week? But of course she had to go to Dublin to be in the tip of the fashion and see what they wear in Grafton Street in the lamplight. She had to get an outfit of immodest fol-the-dols to be a disgrace in the chapel every Sunday, and give room to the missioners when they come to say things that may have an injurious effect upon poor dressmakers like myself who strive to earn a living as decently as we can."

This harangue was almost unnoticed by John Brennan. It was a failing of his mother to be always speaking thus in terms of her trade. He knew that if Miss Kerr had come here with her new dress, fine words and encomiums would now be spoken of her in this room. But it was his mother who was speaking—and he was thinking of the girl who had filled his vision.

And his mother was still talking:

"That Ulick Shannon, I hate him. I wish you wouldn't let yourself be seen along with him. It is not good for you, *avic machree*. Of course I know the kind of talk you do be having, son. About books and classes and the tricks and pranks of you at college. Ah, dear, I know; but I'd rather to God it was any other one in the whole world. I'm fearing in me heart that there's a black, black side to him. It's well known that he bees always drinking in

Garradrimna, and now see how he's after striking up with the schoolmistress one. Maybe 'tis what he'd try to change you sometime, for as sure as you're there I'm afraid and afraid. And to think after all I have prayed for you through all the years, upon me two bare knees in the lonely nights, if an affliction should come."

"What affliction, mother? What is it?"

He came nearer, and gazing deep into her face saw that there were tears in her eyes. Her eyes were shining like deep wells.

"Ah, this, son. If it should ever come that you did not think well to do me wish, after all I have done—"

She checked herself of a sudden, and it was some moments before John replied. He, too, was thinking of Ulick Shannon. There was a side to his friend that he did not like. Yesterday he had not liked him. There were moments when he had hated him. But that mood and the reason for it seemed to have passed from him during the night. It was a far thing now, and Ulick Shannon was as he had been to John, who could not think ill of him. Yet it was curious that his mother should be hinting at things which, if he allowed his mind to dwell upon them at all, must bring back his feelings of yesterday.... But he felt that he must speak well of his friend.

"Ah, sure there is nothing, mother. You are only fancying queer things. At college I have to meet hundreds of fellows. He's not a bad chap, and I like speaking to him. It is lonely here without such intercourse. He realizes keenly how people are always talking of him, how the smallest action of his is construed and constructed in a hundred different ways, until he's driven to do wild things out of very defiance to show what he thinks of the mean people of the valley and their opinion of him—"

"They're not much, I know—"

"But at heart, I think, he's somehow like myself, and I can't help liking him."

"All the same he shouldn't be going with a girl and, especially, a little chit of a schoolmistress like this one, for I can't stand her."

Why did she continue to hammer so upon the pulse of his thought?... With bowed head he began to drift out of the room. Why had she driven him to think now of Rebecca Kerr?... He was already in the sunlight.

To-day he would not go towards the lake, but up through the high green fields of Scarden. He was taking *The Imitation of Christ* with him, and, under the shade of some noble tree, it was his intention to turn his thoughts to God and away from the things of life.

It seemed grand to him, with a grandeur that had more than a touch of the color of Heaven, to be ascending cool slopes through the green, soft grass and to be looking down upon the valley at its daily labor. The potatoes and turnips still required attention. He saw men move patiently behind their horses over the broken fields of red earth beneath the fine, clear clay, and thought that here surely was the true vocation of him who would incline himself unto God.... But how untrue was this fancy when one came to consider the real personality of these tillers of the soil? There was not one of whom Mrs. Brennan could not tell an ugly story. Not one who did not consider it his duty to say uncharitable things of Ulick Shannon and Rebecca Kerr. Not one who would not have danced with gladness if a great misfortune had befallen John Brennan, and made a holiday in Garradrimna if anything terrible had happened to any one within the circle of their acquaintance.

John Brennan's attention was now attracted by a man who moved with an air of proprietorship among a field of sheep. He was a tall man in black, moving darkly among the white crowd of the sheep, counting them leisurely and allowing his mind to dwell upon the pageant of their perfect whiteness. He seemed to be reckoning their value as the pure yield of his pastures. Here was another aspect of the fields.... The man in black was coming towards him with long strides.

It took John some moments to realize that he had strayed into the farm of the Shannons and that this was Myles Shannon who was coming over to meet him.... He was a fine, clean man seen here amid the rich surroundings of his own fields. But he had advanced far into bachelorhood, and the russet was beginning to go out of his cheeks. It seemed a pity of the world that he had not married, for just there, hidden behind the billowy trees, was the fine house to which he might have brought home a wife and reared up a family to love and honor him in his days. But his romance had been shattered by a piece of villainy which had leaped out from the darkness of the valley. And now he was living here alone. But he was serenely independent, exhibiting a fine contempt, as well he might, for the mean strugglers around him. He took his pleasures here by himself in this quiet house among the trees. Had he been asked to name them, he could have told you in three words—books and drink. Not that they entered into his life to any great extent, for he was a wise man even in his indulgence.... But who was there to see him or know since he did not choose to publish himself in Garradrimna? And there was many a time when he worked himself into a great frenzy while brooding over the story of his dead brother Henry, and his own story, and Nan Byrne.... Even now he was thinking darkly of Nan Byrne as he came forward to meet her son across his own field.

"Good-day, Mr. Brennan!" he said affably. He had no personal grudge against this young man, but his scheme of revenge inevitably included him, for it was through John Brennan, her son, that Nan Byrne now hoped to aspire, and it was him she hoped to embody as a monument of her triumph over destructive circumstances before the people of the valley.

John went forward and shook the hand of Mr. Shannon with deference.

A fine cut of a man, surely, this Myles Shannon, standing here where he might be clearly viewed. He appeared as a survival from the latter part of the Victorian era. He was still mutton-chopped and mustachioed after the fashion of those days. He wore a long-tailed black coat like a morning-coat. His waistcoat was of the same material. Across the expanse of it extended a wide gold chain, from which dangled a bunch of heavy seals. These shook and jingled with his every movement. His trousers were of a dark gray material, with stripes, which seemed to add to the height and erectness of his figure. His tall, stiff collar corrected the thoughtful droop of his head, and about it was tastefully fixed a wide black tie of shiny silk which reached down underneath his low-cut waistcoat. His person was surmounted by an uncomfortable-looking bowler hat with a very hard, curly brim.

When he smiled, as just now, his teeth showed in even, fine rows and exhibited some of the cruelty of one who has allowed his mind to dwell darkly upon a passionate purpose. But the ring of his laugh was hearty enough and had the immediate effect of dispelling suspicions of any sinister purpose.

He said he was glad to see how his casual suggestion, made upon the day they had journeyed down from Dublin together, had borne fruit, that Mr. Brennan and his nephew, Ulick, had so quickly become friends.

John thanked him, and began to speak in terms of praise about Ulick Shannon.

Mr. Shannon again bared his even, white teeth in a smile as he listened.... A strong friendship, with its consequent community of inclinations, had already been established. And he knew his nephew.

"He's a clever chap, I'll admit, but he's so damned erratic. He seems bent upon crushing the experience of a lifetime into a few years. Why I'm a man, at the ripened, mellow period of life, and it's a fact that he could teach me things about Dublin and all that."

John Brennan was uncertain in what way he should confirm this, but at last he managed to stammer out:

"Ulick is very clever!"

"He's very fond of Garradrimna, and I think he's very fond of the girls."

"It's so dull around here compared with Dublin."

John appeared a fool by the side of this man of the world, who was searching him with a look as he spoke again:

"It's all right for a young fellow to gain his experience as early as he can, but he's a bit too fond of his pleasure. He's going a bit too far."

John put on a strained look of advocacy, but he spoke no word.

"He's not a doctor yet, and even then his living would not be assured; and do ye know what he had the cheek to come telling me the other night—

"'I've got infernally fond of that little girl,' he says.

"'What girl?' I asked in amazement.

"'Why, that schoolmistress—Rebecca Kerr. I'm "gone" about her. I'm in love with her. She's not at all like any of the others.'"

Myles Shannon, with his keen eyes, saw the sudden light of surprise that leaped into the eyes of John Brennan. The passion of his hatred and the joy of his cruelty were stirred, and he went on to develop the plot of the story he had invented.

"And what for," said I to him, "are you thinking of any girl in that way. I, as your guardian, am able to tell you that you are not in a position to marry. Surely you're not going to ruin this girl, or allow her to ruin you. Besides she is only a strolling schoolmistress from some unknown part of Donegal, and you are one of the Shannon family. 'But I'm "gone" about her,' was what Ulick said. How was I to argue against such a silly statement?"

The color was mounting ever higher on John Brennan's cheeks.

But the relentless man went on playing with him.

"Of course I have not seen her, but, by all accounts, she's a pretty girl and possesses the usual share of allurements. Is not that so?"

"She's very nice."

"And, do you know what? It has come to me up here, although I may seem to be a hermit among the fields who takes no interest in the world, that you have been seen walking down the valley road together. D'ye remember yesterday morning, eh?"

John was blushing still, and a kind of sickly smile made his fine face look queer. All kinds of expressions were trying to form themselves upon his tongue, yet not one of them could he manage to articulate.

"Not that I blame a young fellow, even one intended for the Church, if he should have a few inclinations that way. But I can see that you are the good friend of my nephew, and indeed it would be a pity if anything came to spoil that friendship, least of all a bit of a girl.... And both of you being the promising young men you are.... It would be terrible if anything like that should come to pass."

Even to this John could frame no reply. But the ear of Mr. Shannon did not desire it, for his eye had seen all that he wished to know. He beheld John Brennan shivering as within the cold and dismal shadows of fatality.... They spoke little more until they shook hands again, and parted amid the dappled grass.

To Myles Shannon the interview had been an extraordinary success.... Yet, quite suddenly, he found himself beginning to think of the position of Rebecca Kerr.

CHAPTER XIX

Outside the poor round of diversions afforded by the valley and her meetings with Ulick Shannon, the days passed uneventfully for Rebecca Kerr. It was a dreary kind of life, wherein she was concerned to avoid as far as possible the fits of depression which sprang out of the quality of her lodgings at Sergeant McGoldrick's.

She snatched a hasty breakfast early in the mornings, scarcely ever making anything like a meal. When she did it was always followed by a feeling of nausea as she went on The Road of the Dead towards the valley school. When she returned after her day's hard work her dinner would be half cold and unappetizing by the red ashy fire. Mrs. McGoldrick would be in the sitting-room, where she made clothes for the children, the sergeant himself probably digging in the garden before the door, his tunic open, his face sweating, and the dirty clay upon his big boots.... He was always certain to shout out some idiotic salutation as she passed in. Then Mrs. McGoldrick would be sure to follow her into the kitchen, a baby upon her left arm and a piece of soiled sewing in her right hand. She was always concerned greatly about the number at school on any particular day, and how Mrs. Wyse was and Miss McKeon, and how the average was keeping up, and if it did not keep up to a certain number would Mrs. Wyse's salary be reduced, and what was the average required for Miss McKeon to get her salary from the Board, and so on.

Sometimes Rebecca would be so sick at heart of school affairs and of this mean, prying woman that no word would come from her, and Mrs. McGoldrick would drift huffily away, her face a perfect study in disappointment. And against those there were times when Rebecca, with a touch of good humor, would tell the most fantastical stories of inspectors and rules and averages and increments and pensions, Mrs. McGoldrick breathless between her "Well, wells!" of amazement.... Then Rebecca would have a rare laugh to herself as she pictured her landlady repeating everything to the sergeant, who would make mental comparisons the while of the curious correspondence existing between those pillars of law and learning, the Royal Irish Constabulary, and the National Teachers of Ireland.

Next day, perhaps, Mrs. McGoldrick would enlarge upon the excellent and suitable match a policeman and a teacher make, and how it is such a general thing throughout the country. She always concluded a discourse of this nature by saying a thing she evidently wished Rebecca to remember:

"Let me tell you this, now—a policeman is the very best match that any girl can make!"

And big louts of young constables would be jumping off high bicycles and calling in the evenings.... This was at the instigation of Mrs. McGoldrick, but they made no impression whatsoever upon Rebecca, even when they arrived in mufti.

In school the ugly, discolored walls which had been so badly distempered by Ned Brennan; the monotony of the maps and desks; the constant sameness of the children's faces. All this was infinitely wearying, but a more subtle and powerful torment arose beyond the hum of the children learning by heart. Rebecca always became aware of it through a burning feeling at the back of her neck. Glancing around she would see that, although presumably intent upon their lessons, many eyes were upon her, peering furtively from behind their books, observing her, forming opinions of her, and concocting stories to tell their parents when they went home. For this was considered an essential part of their training—the proper satisfaction of their elders' curiosity. It was one of the reasons why the bigger girls were sent to school. They escaped the drudgery of house and farm because they were able to return with fresh stories from the school every evening. Thus were their faculties for lying and invention brought into play. They feared Mrs. Wyse, and so these faculties came to be trained in full strength upon Rebecca. As she moved about the school-room, she was made the constant object of their scrutiny. They would stare at her with their mean, impudent eyes above the top edges of their books. Then they would withdraw them behind the opened pages and sneer and concoct. And it was thus the forenoon would pass until the half-hour allowed for recreation, when she would be thrown back upon the company of Mrs. Wyse and Monica McKeon. No great pleasure was in store for her here, for their conversation was always sure to turn upon the small affairs of the valley.

There was something so ingenuous about the relations of Rebecca and Ulick Shannon that neither of the two women had the courage to comment upon the matter openly. But the method they substituted was a greater torture. In the course of half an hour they would suggest a thousand hateful things.

"I heard Ulick Shannon was drunk last night, and having arguments with people in Garradrimna," Miss McKeon would say.

Mrs. Wyse would snatch up the words hastily. "Is that so? Oh, he's going to the bad. He'll never pass his exams, never!"

"Isn't it funny how his uncle does not keep better control of him. Why he lets him do what he likes?"

"Control, is it? It doesn't look much like control indeed to see him encouraging his dead brother's son to keep the company he favors. Indeed and indeed it gives me a kind of a turn when I see him going about with Nan

Byrne's son, young John Brennan, who's going on to be a priest. Well, I may tell you that it is 'going on' he is, for his mother as sure as you're there'll never see him saying his first Mass. Now I suppose the poor rector of the college in England where he is hasn't a notion of his antecedents. The cheek of it indeed! But what else could you expect from the likes of Nan Byrne? Indeed I have a good mind to let the ecclesiastical authorities know all, and if nothing turns up from the Hand of God to right the matter, sure I'll have to do it myself. Bedad then I will!"

"Musha, the same John Brennan doesn't look up to much, and they say Ulick Shannon can wind him around his little finger. He'll maybe make a *lad* of him before the end of the summer holidays."

"I can't understand Myles Shannon letting them go about together so openly unless he's enjoying the whole thing as a sneer. But it would be more to his credit indeed to have found other material for his fun than a blood relation. I'm surprised at him indeed, and he knowing what he knows about Nan Byrne and his brother Henry."

With slight variations of this theme falling on her ears endlessly Rebecca was compelled to endure the torture of this half hour every day. No matter what took place in the valley Monica would manage, somehow, to drag the name of Ulick into it. If it merely happened to be a copy of the *Irish Independent* they were looking at, and if they came upon some extraordinary piece of news, Monica would say:

"Just like a thing that Ulick Shannon would do, isn't it?"

And if they came across a photo in the magazine section, Monica would say again:

"Now wouldn't you imagine that gentleman has a look of Ulick Shannon?"

Rebecca had become so accustomed to all this that, overleaping its purpose, it ceased to have any considerable effect upon her. She had begun to care too much for Ulick to show her affection in even the glimpse of an aspect to the two who were trying to discover her for the satisfaction of their spite. It was thus that she remained a puzzle to her colleagues, and Monica in particular was at her wit's end to know what to think. At the end of the half hour she was always in a deeper condition of defeat than before it began, and went out to the Boys' School with only one idea warming her mind, that, some day, she might have the great laugh at Rebecca Kerr. She knew that it is not possible for a woman to hide her feelings forever, even though she thought this one cute surely, cute beyond all the suggestion of her innocent exterior.

Towards the end of each day Rebecca was thrown altogether with the little ones who, despite all the entreaties of their parents, had not yet come very far away from Heaven. She found great pleasure in their company and in their innocent stories. For example:

"Miss Kerr, I was in the wood last night. With the big bear and the little bear in the wood. I went into the wood, and there was the big bear walking round and round the wood after the little bear, and the big bear was walking round and round the wood."

"I was in America last night, and I saw all the motor cars ever were, and people riding on horses, and the highest, whitest buildings ever were, and people going to Mass—big crowds of people going to Mass."

"My mammy brought me into the chapel last night, and I saw God. I was talking to God and He was asking me about you. I said: 'Miss Kerr is nice, so she is.' I said this to God, but God did not answer me. I asked God again did He know Miss Kerr who teaches in the valley school, and He said He did, and I said again: 'Miss Kerr is nice, so she is.' But He went away and did not answer me."

Rebecca would enter into their innocence and so experience the happiest hours of the day.

She would be recalled from her rapt condition by the harsh voice of Mrs. Wyse shouting an order to one of the little girls in her class, this being a hint that she herself was not attending to her business.

But soon the last blessed period of the day would come, the half hour devoted to religious instruction. She found a pleasure in this task, for she loved to hear the little children at their prayers. Sometimes she would ask them to say for her the little prayer she had taught them:

"O God, I offer up this prayer for the poor intentions of Thy servant Rebecca Kerr, that they may be fulfilled unto the glory of Thy Holy Will. And that being imperfect, she may approach to Thy Perfection through the Grace and Mercy of Jesus Christ, Our Lord."

She would feel a certain happiness for a short space after this, at least while the boisterous business of taking leave of the school was going forward. But once upon the road she would be meeting people who always stared at her strangely, and passing houses with squinting windows.... Then would come a heavy sense of depression, which might be momentarily dispelled by the appearance of John Brennan either coming or going upon the road. For a while she had considered this happening coincidental, but of late it had been borne in upon her that it was very curious he should appear daily at the same time.... The silly boy, and he with his grand purpose before him.... She would smile upon him very pleasantly, and fall into chat sometimes, but only for a few minutes. She looked upon herself as being ever so much wiser. And she thought it queer that he should find an attraction for his eyes in her form as it moved before him down the road. She always fancied that she felt low and mean within herself while his eyes were upon her.... But he would be forever coming out of his mother's cottage to meet her thus upon the road.

After dinner in the house of Sergeant McGoldrick she would betake herself to her little room. It would be untidy after the hurry in which she had left it, and now she would set about putting it to rights. This would occupy her half an hour or more. Then there would be a few letters to be written, to her people away in Donegal and to some of the companions of her training college days. She kept up a more or less regular correspondence with about half-a-dozen of these girls. Her letters were all after the frivolous style of their schooldays. To all of them she imparted the confidence that she had met "a very nice fellow" here in Garradrimna, but that the place was so lonely, and how there was "nothing like a girl friend."

"Ah, Anna," she would write, or "Lily" or "Lena," "There's surely nothing after all like a girl friend."

After tea she would put on one of her tidiest hats, and taking the letters with her go towards the Post Office of Garradrimna. This was a torture, for always the eyes of the old, bespectacled maid were upon her, looking into her mind, as she stood waiting for her stamps outside the ink-stained counter. And, further, she always felt that the doors and windows of the village were forever filled with eyes as she went by them. Her neck and face would burn until she took the road that led out past the old castle of the De Lacys. There was a footpath which took one to the west gate of the demesne of the Moores. The Honorable Reginald Moore was the modern lord of Garradrimna. It was this way she would go, meeting all kinds of stragglers from the other end of the parish. People she did not know and who did not know her, queer, dark men coming into Garradrimna through the high evening in quest of porter.

"Fine evening, miss!" they would say.

Once on the avenue her little walk became a golden journey for Ulick always met her when she came this way. It was their custom to meet here or on The Road of the Dead. But this was their favorite spot, where the avenue led far into the quiet woods. A scurrying-away of rabbits through the undergrowth would announce their approach to one another.

Many were the happy talks they had here, of books and of decent life beyond the boorishness of Garradrimna. She had given him *The Poems of Tennyson* in exchange for *The Daffodil Fields*. Tastefully illuminated in red ink on the fly-leaf he had found her "favorite lines" from Tennyson, whom she considered "exquisite":

Glitter like a storm of fire-flies tangled in a silver braid."

Cursed be the gold that gilds the straightened forehead of the fool."

Many an evening by the waters did we watch the stately ships,

And our spirits rushed together at the touching of the lips."

These had made him smile, and then he did not read any more of Tennyson.... He was fond of telling her about the younger Irish poets and of quoting passages from their poems. Now it would be a line or so from Colum or Stephens, again a verse from Seumas O'Sullivan or Joseph Campbell. Continually he spoke with enthusiasm of the man they called Æ.... She found it difficult to believe that such men could be living in Ireland at the present time.

"And would you see them about Dublin?"

"Yes, you'd see them often."

"*Real* poets?"

"Real poets surely. But of course they have earthly interests as well. One is a farmer—"

"A farmer!!!"

This she found it hardest of all to believe, for the word "farmer" made her see so clearly the sullen men with the dirty beards who came in the white roads every evening to drink in Garradrimna. There was no poetry in them.

Often they would remain talking after this fashion until night had filled up all the open spaces of the woods. They would feel so far away from life amid the perfect stillness.... Their peace was rudely shattered one night by a sudden breaking away from them through the withered branches.... Instantly Ulick knew that this was some loafer sent to spy on them from Garradrimna, and Rebecca clung to him for protection.

Occasionally through the summer a lonely wailing had been heard in the woods of Garradrimna at the fall of night. Men drinking in the pubs would turn to one another and say:

"The Lord save us! Is that the *Banshee* I hear crying for one of the Moores? She cries like that always when one of them dies, they being a noble family. Maybe the Honorable Reginald is after getting his death at last in some whore-house in London."

"Arrah not at all, man, sure that's only Anthony Shaughness and he going crying through the woods for drink, the poor fellow!"

But the sound had ceased to disturb them for Anthony Shaughness had found an occupation at last. This evening he came running down from the woods into McDermott's bar, the loose soles of his boots slapping against the cobbles of the yard. Josie Guinan went up to him excitedly when he entered.

"Well?" This in a whisper as their heads came close together over the counter.

"Gimme a drink? I'm choked with the running, so I am!"

"Tell me did you see them first, or not a sup you'll get. Don't be so smart now, Anthony Shaughness!"

"Oh, I saw them all right. Gimme the drink?"

She filled the drink, making it overflow the glass in her hurry.

"Well?"

"Bedad I saw them all right. Heard every word they were saying, so I did, and everything! It was the devil's father to find them, so it was, they were that well hid in the woods.... Gimme another sup, Josie?"

"Now, Anthony?"

"Ah, but you don't know all I have to tell ye!"

Again she overflowed the glass in her mounting excitement.

"Well?"

———————————————

CHAPTER XX

The summer was beginning to wane, August having sped to its end. The schools had given vacation, and Rebecca Kerr had gone away from the valley to Donegal. Ulick Shannon had returned to Dublin. This was the uneventful season in the valley. Mrs. Brennan, finding little to talk about, had grown quiet in herself. Ned had taken his departure to Ballinamult, where he was engaged in putting some lead upon the roof of the police-barracks. He was drinking to his heart's content, she knew, and would come home to her without a penny saved against his long spell of idleness or the coming rigors of the winter. But she was thankful for the present that he had removed himself from the presence of his son. It was not good for such a son to be compelled to look upon such a father. She had prayed for this blessing and lo! it had come. And it extended further. Ulick Shannon too was gone from the valley, and so she was no longer annoyed by seeing him in company with her son. Their friendship had progressed through the months of July and August, and she was aware that they had been seen together many times in Garradrimna. She did not know the full truth but, as on the first occasion, the lake could tell. Rebecca Kerr was gone, and so there was no need to speak of this strange girl for whom some wild feeling had enkindled a flame of hatred within her. Thus was she left in loneliness and peace to dwell upon the wonder of her son. He seemed more real to her during these quiet days, nearer perhaps, than he had ever been since she had first begun to dream her great dream.

Of late he had taken to his room upstairs, where he did a little study daily. "So that it won't be altogether too strange when I go back again to college," he told her on more than one occasion when she besought him not to be blinding his eyes while there was yet leisure to rest them. There were times during the long quiet day in the house when her flood of love for him would so well up within her that she would call him down for no other reason than that she might have the great pleasure of allowing her eyes to rest upon him for a short space only. She would speak no word at all, so fearful would she be of disturbing the holy peace which fell between them. In the last week of his present stay in the valley this happened so often that it became a little wearying to John, who had begun to experience a certain feeling of independence in his own mind. It pained him greatly now that his mother should love him so.... And there were many times when he longed to be back in his English college, with his books and friends, near opportunities to escape from the influences which had conspired to change him.

One morning, after his mother had gazed upon him in this way, he came out of the house and leaned over the little wicket gate to take a look at the day. It was approaching Farrell McGuinness's time to be along with the post, and

John expected him to have a letter from the rector of the College giving some directions as to the date of return. Yet he was not altogether so anxious to return as he had been towards the ends of former vacations.... At last Farrell McGuinness appeared around the turn of the road. His blue uniform was dusty, and he carried his hard little cap in his hand. He dismounted from his red bicycle and took two letters out of his bag. He smirked obviously as he performed this action. John glanced in excitement at the letters. One was addressed in the handwriting of his friend Ulick Shannon and the other in the handwriting of a girl. It was this last one that had caused Farrell McGuinness to smirk so loudly.

"'Tis you that has the times, begad!" he said to John as he mounted his red bicycle and went on up the road, fanning his hot brow with his hard cap.

Mrs. Brennan came to the door to hear tidings of the letters from her son, but John was already hurrying down through the withering garden, tearing open both letters simultaneously.

"Who are they from?" she called out.

"From Ulick Shannon."

"And th'other one?"

"From a chap in the college," he shouted across his shoulder, lying boldly to her for the first time in his life. But if only she could see the confusion upon his face?

She went back into the sewing-room, a feeling of annoyance showing in the deep lines about her eyes. It seemed strange that he had not rushed immediately into the house to tell her what was in the letters, strange beyond all how he had not seen his way to make that much of her.

Down the garden John was reading Rebecca Kerr's letter first, for it was from her that the letter from "one of the chaps in the college" had come.

It told of how she was spending her holidays at a seaside village in Donegal. "It is even far quieter than Garradrimna and the valley. I go down to the sea in the mornings, but it is only to think and dream. The sea is just like one big lake, more lonely by far than the lake in the valley. This is surely the loneliest place you could imagine, but there is a certain sense of peace about it that is quite lovely. It is some distance from my home, and it is nice to be amongst people who have no immense concern for your eternal welfare. I like this, and so I have avoided making acquaintances here. But next week I am expecting a very dear friend to join me, and so, I dare say, my holidays will have a happy ending after all. I suppose you will have gone from the valley when I go back in October. And it will be the dreary place then...." She signed herself, "Yours very sincerely, Rebecca Kerr."

His eyes were dancing as he turned to read Ulick Shannon's letter.... In the opening passages it treated only in a conventional way of college affairs, but suddenly he was upon certain lines which to his mind seemed so blackly emphasized:

"Now I was just beginning to settle back into the routine of things when who should come along but Miss Kerr? She was looking fine. She stayed a few days here in Dublin, and I spent most of them with her. I gave her the time of her life, the poor little thing! Theaters every night, and all the rest of it. She was just lost for a bit of enjoyment. Grinding away, you know, in those cursed National Schools from year's end to year's end. Do you know what it is, John? I am getting fonder and fonder of that girl. She is the best little soul in all the world.

"She is spending her holidays up in some God-forsaken village in Donegal. Away from her people and by herself, you know. She has a girl friend going to see her next week. You will not be able to believe it probably—*but I am the girl friend.*"

He read them and re-read them, these two letters which bore so intimately upon one another and which, through the coincidence of their arrival together, held convincing evidence of the dramatic moment that had arrived in the adventure of those two lives.

He became filled by an aching feeling that made him shiver and grow weak as if with some unknown expectation.... Yet why was he so disturbed in his mind as to this happening; what had he to do with it? He was one whose life must be directed away from such things. But the vision of Rebecca Kerr would be filling his eyes forever. And why had she written to him? Why had she so graphically pictured her condition of loneliness wherein he might enter and speak to her? His acquaintance with her was very slight, and yet he desired to know her beyond all the knowledge and beauty of the world.... And to think that it was Ulick Shannon who was now going where he longed to go.

A heavy constraint came between him and his mother during the remaining days. He spoke little and moved about in meditation like one fearful of things about to happen. But she fondly fancied as always that he was immersed in contemplation of the future she had planned for him. She never saw him setting forth into the autumn fields, a book in his hand, that she did not fancy the look of austere aloofness upon his face to be the expression of a priest reading his office. But thoughts of this kind were far from his mind in the fields or by the little wicket gate across which he often leaned, his eyes fixed upon the white, hard road which seemed to lead nowhere.

The day of his release at last came. Now that Ned was away from her, working in Ballinamult, she had managed to scrape together the price of another motor drive to Kilaconnaghan, but it was in the misfortune of things that Charlie Clarke's car should have been engaged for the very day of John's departure by the Houlihans of Clonabroney. It worried her greatly that she could not have this piece of grandeur upon this second occasion. Her intense devotion to religious literature had made her superstitious to a distressing degree. It appeared to her as an omen across the path of John and her own magnification. But John did not seem to mind.

It was notable that through his advance into contemplation he had triumphed over the power of the valley to a certain extent. So long as his mind had been altogether absorbed in thought of the priesthood he had moved about furtively, a fugitive, as it were, before the hateful looks of the people of the valley and the constant stare of the squinting windows. Now he had come into a little tranquillity and his heart was not without some happiness in the enjoyment of his larger vision.... And yet he was far from being completely at peace.

As he sat driving with his mother in the ass-trap to Kilaconnaghan, on his way back to the grand college in England, his doubts were assailing him although he was so quiet, to all seeming, sitting there. Those who passed them upon the road never guessed that this pale-faced young man in black was at war with his soul.... Few words passed between him and his mother, for the constraint of the past week had not yet been lifted. She was beginning to feel so lonely, and she was vexed with herself that the period of his stay in the valley had not been all she had dreamt of making it. It had been disappointing to a depressing extent, and now especially in its concluding stage. This sad excursion in the little ass-trap, without any of the pomp and circumstance which John so highly deserved, was a poor, mean ending.

He was running over in his mind the different causes which had given this vacation its unusual character. First there came remembrance of his journey down from Dublin with Mr. Myles Shannon, who had then suggested the friendship with his nephew Ulick. Springing out of this thought was a very vivid impression of Garradrimna, that ugly place which he had discovered in its true colors for the first time; its vile set of drunkards and the few secret lapses it had occasioned him. Then there was his father, that fallen and besotted man whom the valley had ruined past all hope. As a more intimate recollection his own doubts of the religious life by the lakeside arose clear before him. And the lake itself seemed very near, for it had been the silent witness of all his moods and conditions, the dead thing that had gathered to itself a full record of his sojourn in the valley. But, above all, there was Rebecca Kerr, whom he had contrived to meet so often as she went from school. It was she who now brought light to all the darkened places of his memory. Her letter to him the other day was the one real thing he had been given to take away from the valley. How he longed to read it again! But his mother's eyes were upon him.... At last he began to have a little thought of the part she had played.

Already they had reached the railway station of Kilaconnaghan. They went together through the little waiting-room, which held sad memories for Mrs. Brennan, and out upon the platform, where a couple of porters leaned against their barrows chewing tobacco. Two or three passengers were sitting around beside their luggage waiting to take the train for Dublin. A few bank clerks from the town were standing in a little group which possessed an imaginary distinction, laughing in a genteel way at a puerile joke from some of the London weekly journals. They were wearing sporting clothes and had fresh fags in their mouths. It was an essential portion of their occupation, this perpetual delight in watching the outgoing afternoon train.

"Aren't they the grand-looking young swells?" said Mrs. Brennan; "I suppose them have the great jobs now?"

"Great!" replied John, quite unconscious of what he said.

He spoke no other word till he took his place in the train. She kissed him through the open window and hung affectionately to his hand.... Then there fluttered in upon them the moment of parting.... Smiling wistfully and waving her hand, she watched the train until it had rounded a curve. She lingered for a moment by the advertisement for Jameson's Whiskey in the waiting-room to wipe her eyes. She began to remember how she had behaved here in this very place on the day of John's home-coming, and of how he had left her standing while he talked to Myles Shannon.... He seemed to have slipped away from her now, and her present thought made her feel that the shadow of the Shannon family, stretching far across her life, had attended his going as it had attended his coming.

She went out to the little waiting ass and, mounting into the trap, drove out of Kilaconnaghan into the dark forest of her fears.

CHAPTER XXI

Through the earlier part of this term at college there was no peace in the mind of John Brennan, and his unsettled state arose, for the most part, from simple remembrance of things that had happened in the valley. Now it was because he could see again, some afternoon in the summer, Rebecca Kerr coming towards him down the road in a brown and white striped dress, that he thought was pretty, and swinging a sun-bonnet by its long cotton strings from her soft, small hand. Or again, some hour he had spent listening to Ulick Shannon as he talked about the things of life which are marked only by the beauty of passion and death. Always, too, with the aid of two letters he still treasured, his imagination would leap towards the creation of a picture—Rebecca and Ulick together in far-off Donegal.

He did not go home at Christmas because it was so expensive to return to Ireland, and in the lonely stretches of the vacation, when all his college friends were away from him, he felt that they must surely be meeting again, meeting and kissing in some quiet, dusky place—Rebecca as he had seen her always and Ulick as he had known him.

Even if he had wished to leave Ulick and Rebecca out of his mind, it would have been impossible, so persistently did his mother refer to both in her letters. There was never a letter which did not contain some allusion to "them two" or "that one" or "that fellow." In February, when the days began to stretch out again, he thought only of the valley coming nearer, with its long period of delight.... Within the fascination of his musing he grew forgetful of his lofty future. Yet there were odd moments when he remembered that he had moved into the valley a very different man at the beginning of last June. The valley had changed him, and might continue to change him when he went there again.

Nothing came to stay the even rise of his yearning save his mother's letters, which were the same recitals at all times of stories about the same people. At no time did he expect to find anything new in them, and so it was all the stronger blow when from one letter leaped out the news that Ulick Shannon had failed to pass his final medical exam., and was now living at home in Scarden House with his uncle Myles. That he had been "expelled from the University and disgraced" was the way she put it. It did not please John to see that she was exulting over what had happened to Ulick while hinting at the same time that there was no fear of a like calamity happening to her son. To him it appeared as not at all such an event as one might exult about. It rather evoked pity and condolence in the thought that it might happen to any man. It might happen to himself. Here surely was a fearful thing—the sudden dread of his return to the valley, a disgrace for life, and his mother a ruined woman in the downfall of her son.... This last letter of hers had brought him to review all the brave thoughts that had come to him by the lakeside, wild thoughts of living his own life, not in the way appointed for him by any other person, but freely, after the bent of his own will. Yet when he came to think of it quietly there was not much he could do in the world with his present education. It seemed to have fitted him only for one kind of life. And his thoughts of the summer might have been only passing distractions which must disappear with the full development of his mind. To think of those ideas ever coming suddenly to reality would be a blow too powerful to his mother. It would kill her. For, with other knowledge, the summer holidays had brought him to see how much she looked forward to his becoming a priest.

Quite unconsciously, without the least effort of his will, he found himself returning to his old, keen interest in his studies. He found himself coming back to his lost peace of mind. He felt somehow that his enjoyment of this grand contentment was the very best way he could flash back his mother's love. Besides it was the best earnest he had of the enjoyment of his coming holidays.

Then the disaster came. The imminence of it had been troubling the rector for a long time. His college was in a state of disintegration, for the Great War had cast its shadow over the quiet walls.

It was a charity college. This was a secret that had been well kept from the people of the valley by Mrs. Brennan. "A grand college in England" was the utmost information she would ever vouchsafe to any inquirer. She had formed a friendly alliance with the old, bespectacled postmistress and made all her things free of charge for keeping close the knowledge of John's exact whereabouts in England. Yet there was never a letter from mother to son or from son to mother that the old maid did not consider it her bounden duty to open and read.

The college had been supported by good people who could find nothing else to do with their money. But, in war-time, charity was diverted into other channels, and its income had consequently dwindled almost to vanishing point. Coupled with this, many of the students had left aside their books and gone into the Army. One morning the rector appeared in the lecture-hall to announce to the remnant that the college was about to be closed for "some time." He meant indefinitely, but the poor man could not put it in that way.

John heard the news with mingled feelings. In a dumb way he had longed for this after his return from the valley, but now he saw in it, not the arrival of a desired event, but a postponement of the great intention that had begun to absorb him again. He was achieving his desire in a way that made it a punishment.... To-morrow he would be going home.... But of course his mother knew everything by this time and was already preparing a welcome for him.

The March evening was gray and cold when he came into the deserted station of Kilaconnaghan. It had been raining ceaselessly since Christmas, and around and away from him stretched the sodden country. He got a porter to take his trunk out to the van and stand it on end upon the platform. Then he went into the waiting-room to meet his mother. But she was not there. Nor was the little donkey and trap outside the station house. Perhaps she was coming to meet him with Charlie Clarke in the grand and holy motor car. If he went on he might meet them coming through Kilaconnaghan. He got the porter to take his box from its place on the platform and put it into the waiting-room. All down through the town there was no sign of them, and when he got out upon the road to Garradrimna and the valley there was no sign of them either. The night had fallen thick and heavy, and John, as he went on through the rain, looked forward to the comforting radiance of Charlie Clarke's headlights suddenly to flash around every corner. But the car did not come and he began to grow weary of tramping through the wet night. All along the way he was meeting people who shouldered up to him and strove to peer into his face as he slipped past. He did not come on to the valley road by way of Garradrimna, but instead by The Road of the Dead, down which he went slopping through great pools at every few yards.

He was very weary when he came at last to the door of his mother's house. Before knocking he had listened for a while to the low hum of her reading to his father. Then he heard her moving to open the door, and immediately she was silhouetted in the lamp-light.

"Is that you, John? We knew you were coming home. We got the rector's letter."

He noticed a queer coldness in her tone.

"I'd rather to God that anything in the world had happened than this. What'll they say now? They'll say you were expelled. As sure as God, they'll say you were expelled!"

He threw himself into the first chair he saw.

"Did any one meet you down the road? Did many meet you from this to Kilaconnaghan?"

He did not answer. This was a curious welcome he was receiving. Yet he noticed that tears were beginning to creep into her eyes, which were also red as if from much recent weeping.

"Oh, God knows, and God knows again, John, I'd rather have died than it should have come to this. And why was it that after all me contriving and after all me praying and good works this bitter cross should have fallen? I don't know. I can't think for what I am being punished and why misfortune should come to you. And what'll they say at all at all? Oh you may depend upon it that it's the worst thing they'll say. But you mustn't tell them that the college is finished. For I suppose it's finished now the way everything is going to be finished before the war. But you mustn't say that. You must say that it is on special holidays you are, after having passed a Special examination. And you must behave as if you were on holidays!"

Such a dreadful anxiety was upon her that she appeared no longer as his mother, the infinitely tender woman he had known. She now seemed to possess none of the pure contentment her loving tenderness should have brought her. She was altogether concerned as to what the people would say and not as to the effect of the happening upon her son's career. He had begun to think of this for himself, but it was not of it that she was now thinking.... She was thinking of herself, of her pride, and that was why she had not come to meet him. And now his clothes were wet and he was tired, for he had walked from Kilaconnaghan in the rain.

Ned Brennan, stirring out of his drunken doze, muttered thickly: "Ah, God blast yourselves and your college, can't you let a fellow have a sleep be the fire after his hard day!"

CHAPTER XXII

John went from the kitchen to a restless night. Soon after daybreak he got up and looked out of the window. The crows had been flying across it darkly since the beginning of the light. He gazed down now towards the stretch of trees about the lake. They were dark figures in the somber picture. He had not seen them since autumn, and even then some of the brightness of summer had lingered with them. Now they looked as if they had been weeping. He could see the lake between the clumps of fir-trees. The water was all dark like the scene in which it was framed. It now beat itself into a futile imitation of billows, into a kind of make-believe before the wild things around that it was an angry sea, holding deep in its caverns the relics of great dooms. But the trees seemed to rock in enjoyment and to join forces with the wild things in tormenting the lake.

John looked at the clock. It was early hours, and there would be no need to go out for a long time. He went back to bed and remained there without sleep, gazing up at the ceiling.... He fell to thinking of what he would have to face in the valley now.... His mother had hinted at the wide scope of it last night when she said that she would rather anything in God's world had happened than this thing, this sudden home-coming.... She was thinking only of her own pride. It was an offense against her pride, he felt, and that was all. It stood to lessen the exalted position which the purpose of his existence gave her before the other women of the valley. But he had begun to feel the importance of his own person in the scheme of circumstance by which he was surrounded. It had begun to appear to him that he mattered somehow; that in some undreamt-of way he might leave his mark upon the valley before he died.

He would go to Mass in Garradrimna this morning. He very well knew how this attendance at morning Mass was a comfort to his mother. He was about to do this thing to please her now. Yet, how was the matter going to affect himself? He would be stared at by the very walls and trees as he went the wet road into Garradrimna; and no matter what position he might take up in the chapel there would be very certain to be a few who would come kneeling together into a little group and, in hushed tones within the presence of their God upon the altar, say:

"Now, isn't that John Brennan I see before me, or can I believe my eyes? Aye, it must be him. Expelled, I suppose. Begad that's great. Expelled! Begad!" If he happened to take the slightest side-glance around, he would catch glimpses of eyes sunk low beneath brows which published expressions midway between pity and contempt, between delight and curiosity.... In some wonderful way the first evidence of his long hoped for downfall would spread throughout the small congregation. Those in front would let their heads or prayerbooks fall beside or behind them, so that they might have an excuse for turning around to view the young man who, in his unfortunate presence here, stood for this glad piece of intelligence. The acolytes serving Father O'Keeffe, and having occasional glimpses of the congregation, would see the black-coated figure set there in contradistinction to Charlie Clarke and the accustomed voteens with the bobbing bonnets. In their wise looks up at him they would seem to communicate the news to the priest.

And although only a very few seconds had elapsed, Father O'Keeffe would have thrown off his vestments and be going bounding towards the Presbytery for his breakfast as John emerged from the chapel. It would be an ostentatious meeting. Although he had neither act nor part in it, nor did he favor it in any way, Father O'Keeffe always desired people to think that it was he who was "doing for Mrs. Brennan's boy beyond in England." ... There would be the usual flow of questions, a deep pursing of the lips, and the sudden creation of a wise, concerned, ecclesiastical look at every answer. Then there was certain to come the final brutal question: "And what are you going to do with yourself meanwhile, is it any harm to ask?" As he continued to stare up vacantly at the ceiling, John could not frame a possible answer to that question. And yet he knew it would be the foremost of Father O'Keeffe's questions.

There would be the hurried crowding into every doorway and into all the squinting windows as he went past. Outwardly there would be smiles of welcome for him, but in the seven publichouses of Garradrimna the exultation would be so great as to make men who had been ancient enemies stand drinks to one another in the moment of gladness which had come upon them with the return of John Brennan.

"'Tis expelled he is like Ulick Shannon. That's as sure as you're there!"

"To be sure he's expelled. And wouldn't any one know he was going to be expelled the same as the other fellow, the way they were conducting themselves last summer, running after gerrls and drinking like hell?"

"And did ye ever hear such nonsense? The idea of him going on for to be a priest!" Then there would be a shaking of wise heads and a coming of wise looks into their faces.

He could see what would happen when he met the fathers of Garradrimna, when he met Padna Padna or Shamesy Golliher. There would be the short, dry laugh from Padna Padna, and a pathetic scrambling of the dimming intelligence to recognize him.

"And is that you, John? Back again! Well, boys-a-day! And isn't it grand that Ulick Shannon is at home these times too? Isn't it a pity about Ulick, for he's a decent fellow? Every bit as decent as his father, Henry Shannon, was, and he was a damned decent fellow. Ah, 'tis a great pity of him to be exshpelled. Aye, *'tis a great pity of any one that does be exshpelled.*"

The meeting with Shamesy Golliher formed as a clearer picture before his mind.

"Arrah me sound man, John, sure I thought you'd be saying the Mass before this time. There's nothing strange in the valley at all. Only 'tis harder than ever to get the rabbits, the weeshy devils! Only for Ulick Shannon I don't know what I'd do for a drink sometimes. But, damn it, he's the decentest fellow.... You're only a few minutes late, sure 'tis only this blessed minute that Miss Kerr's gone on to the school.... And you could have been chatting with her so grandly all the way!"

That John Brennan should be thinking after this fashion, creating all those little scenes before the eye of his mind and imagining their accompanying conversations, was indicative of the way the valley and the village had forced their reality upon him last summer. But this pictured combination of incidents was intensified by a certain morbid way of dwelling upon things his long spells of meditation by the lake had brought him. Yet he knew that even all his clear vision of the mean ways of life around him would not act as an incentive to combat them but, most extraordinary to imagine, as a sort of lure towards the persecution of their scenes and incidents.

"It must be coming near time to rise for Mass," he said aloud to himself, as he felt that he had been quite a long time giving himself up to speculations in which there was no joy.

There was a tap upon the door. It was his mother calling him, as had been her custom during all the days of his holiday times. The door opened and she came into the room. Her manner seemed to have changed somewhat from the night before. The curious look of tenderness she had always displayed while gazing upon him seemed to have struggled back into her eyes. She came and sat by the bedside and, for a few moments, both were silent.

"'Tis very cold this morning, mother," was the only thing John could think of saying.

A slight confusion seemed to have come upon her since her entrance to the room. Without any warning by a word, she suddenly threw her arms about him as he lay there on the bed and covered his face with kisses. He was amazed, but her kisses seemed to hurt him.... It must have been years and years since she had kissed him like this, and now he was a man.... When she released him so that he could look up at her he saw that she was crying.

"I'm sorry about last night, John," she said. "I'm sorry, darling; but surely I could not bring myself to do it. Even for a few hours I wanted to keep them from knowing. I even wanted to keep your father from knowing. So I did not tell him until I heard your poor, wet foot come sopping up to the door. He did not curse much then, for he seems to have begun to feel a little respect for you. But the curses of him all through the night were enough to lift the roof off the house. Oh, he's the terrible man, for all me praying and all me reading to him of good, holy books; and 'tis no wonder for all kinds of misfortune to fall, though God between us and all harm, what am I saying at all?... It was the hard, long walk down the wet, dark road from Kilaconnaghan last night, and it pained me every inch of the way. If it hurt your feet and your limbs, *avic*, remember that your suffering was nothing to the pain that plowed through your mother's heart all the while you were coming along to this house.... But God only knows I couldn't. I couldn't let them see me setting off into the twilight upon the little ass, and I going for me son. I even went so far as to catch the little ass and yoke him, and put on the grand clothes I was decked out in when I met you last June with the motor. But somehow I hadn't the heart for the journey this time, and you coming home before you were due. I couldn't let them see me! I couldn't let them see me, so I couldn't!"

"But it is not my fault, mother. I have not brought it about directly by any action of mine. It comes from the changed state of everything on account of the Great War. You may say it came naturally."

"Ah, sure I know that, dear, I know it well, and don't be troubling yourself. In the letter of the rector before the very last one didn't he mention the change of resigned application that had at last come to you, and that you had grown less susceptible—I think that is the grand word he used—aye, less susceptible to distractions and more quiet in your mind? And I knew as well as anything that it was coming to pass so beautifully, that all the long prayers I had said for you upon me two bare, bended knees were after being heard at last, and a great joy was just beginning to come surging into me heart when the terrible blow of the last letter fell down upon me. But sure I used to be having the queerest dreams, and I felt that nothing good was going to happen when Ulick Shannon came down here expelled from the University in Dublin. You used to be a great deal in his company last summer, and mebbe there was some curse put upon the both of you together. May God forgive me, but I hate that young fellow like poison. I don't know rightly why it is, but it vexes me to see him idling around the way he is after what's happened to him. Bragging about being expelled he bees every day in McDermott's of Garradrimna. And his uncle Myles is every bit as bad, going to keep him at home until the end of next summer. 'To give him time to think of things,' he says. 'I'm going to find a use for him,' he says to any one that asks him, 'never you fear!' Well, begad, 'tis a grand thing not to know what to do with your money like the Shannons of Scarden Hill.... But sure I'm talking and talking. 'Tis what I came in to tell you now of the plan I have been making up all night. If we let them see that we're lying down under this misfortune we're bet surely. We must put a brave face upon it. You must make a big show-off that you're after getting special holidays for some great, successful examination you've passed ahead of any one else in the college. I'll let on I'm delighted, and be mad to tell it to every customer that comes into the sewing-room. But you must help me; you must go about saying hard things of Ulick Shannon that's after being expelled, for that's the very best way you can do it. He'll mebbe seek your company like last year, but you must let him see for certain that you consider yourself a deal above him. But you mustn't be so quiet and go moping so much about the lake as you used to. You must go about everywhere, talking of yourself and what you're going to be. Now you must do all this for my sake—won't you, John?"

His tremulous "yes" was very unenthusiastic and seemed to hold no great promise of fulfilment. These were hard things his mother was asking him to do, and he would require some time to think them over.... But even now he wondered was it in him to do them at all. The attitude towards Ulick Shannon which she now proposed would be a curious thing, for they had been the best of friends.

"And while you're doing this thing for me, John, I'll be going on with me plans for your future. It was me, and me only, that set up this beautiful plan of the priesthood as the future I wanted for you. I got no one to help me, I can tell you that. Only every one to raise their hands against me. And in spite of all that I carried me plan to what success the rector spoke of in his last letter. And even though this shadow has fallen across it, me son and meself between us are not going to let it be the end. For I want to see you a priest, John. I want to see you a priest before I die. God knows I want to see that before I die. Nan Byrne's son a priest before she dies!"

Her speech mounted to such a pitch of excitement that towards the end it trailed away into a long, frenzied scream. It awoke Ned Brennan where he dozed fitfully in the next room, and he roared out:

"Ah, what the hell are yous gosthering and croaking about in there at this hour of the morning, the two of yous? It'd be serving you a lot better to be down getting me breakfast, Nan Byrne!"

She came away very quietly from the bedside of her son and left the room. John remained for some time thinking over the things she had been saying. Then he rose wearily and went downstairs. It was only now he noticed that his mother had dried his clothes. It must have taken her a good portion of the night to do this. His boots, which had been so wet and muddy after his walk from Kilaconnaghan, were now polished to resplendence and standing clean and dry beside the fire. The full realization of these small actions brought a fine feeling of tenderness into his mind.... He quickly prepared himself to leave the house. She observed him with concern as she went about cooking the breakfast for her man.

"You're not going to Mass this morning, are ye, John?"

"Oh, no!" he replied with a nervous quickness. "Our chat delayed me. It is now past nine."

"Ah, dear, sure I never thought while I was talking. The last time I kept you it was the morning after the concert, and even then you were in time for 'half-past eight'.... But sure, anyhow, you're too tired this morning."

"I'm going for a little walk before breakfast."

The words broke in queerly upon the thought she had just expressed, but his reason was nothing more than to avoid his father, who would be presently snapping savagely at his breakfast in the kitchen.

The wet road was cheerless and the bare trees and fields were cold and lonely. Everything was in contrast to the mood in which he had known it last summer. It seemed as if he would never know it in that mood again. Now that he had returned it was a poor thing and very small beside the pictures his dream had made.... He was wandering down The Road of the Dead and there was a girl coming towards him. He knew it was Rebecca Kerr, and this meeting did not appear in the least accidental.

She was dressed, as he had not previously seen her, in a heavy brown coat, a thick scarf about her throat and a pretty velvet cap which hid most of her hair. Her small feet were well shod in strong boots, and she came radiantly down the wet road. A look of surprise sprang into her eyes when she saw him, and she seemed uncertain of herself as they stopped to speak.

"Back again?" she said, not without some inquisitive surprise in her tones.

"Yes, another holiday," he said quickly.

"Nothing wrong?" she queried.

"Well, well, no; but the college has closed down for the period of the war."

"That is a pity."

He laughed a queer, excited little laugh, in which there did not seem to be any mirth or meaning. Then he picked himself up quickly.

"You won't tell anybody?"

"What about?"

"This that I have told you, about the college."

"Oh, dear no!" she replied very quickly, as if amazed and annoyed that he should have asked her to respect this little piece of information as a confidence. And she had not reckoned on meeting him at all. Besides she had not spoken so many words to him since the morning after the concert.

She lifted her head high and went on walking between the muddy puddles on the way to the valley school.

John felt somewhat crushed by her abruptness, especially after what he had told her. And where was the fine resolve with which his mother had hoped to infuse him of acting a brave part for her sake before the people of the valley?

CHAPTER XXIII

Myles Shannon and his nephew Ulick sat at breakfast in the dining-room of the big house among the trees. The *Irish Times* of the previous day's date was crackling in the elder man's hand.

"Did you ever think of joining the Army, Ulick? It is most extraordinary, the number of ne'er-do-wells who manage to get commissions just now. Why I think there should be no bother at all if you tried. With your knowledge I fancy you could get into the R.A.M.C. It is evidently infernally easy. I suppose your conduct at the University would have nothing to do with your chances of acceptance or rejection?"

"Oh, not at all."

"I thought not."

"But I fancied, uncle, that when I came down here from Dublin I had done with intending myself to kill people. That is, with joining any combination for purposes of slaughter."

Myles Shannon lifted his eyes from the paper and smiled. Evidently he did not appreciate the full, grim point of the joke, but he rather fancied there was something subtle about it, and it was in that quiet and venerable tradition of humorous things his training had led him to enjoy. This was one of the reasons why, even though a Catholic and a moderate Nationalist, he had remained a devoted reader of the *Irish Times*. He was conservative even in his humor.

"But in Army medical work, however, there is always the compensating chance of the gentleman with the license to kill getting killed himself," continued Ulick.

His lips closed now, for he had at last come to the end of his joke. The conversation lapsed, and Mr. Shannon went on with his reading. Ulick had been to Garradrimna on the previous evening, and he was acutely conscious of many defects in his own condition and in the condition of the world about him this morning. His thoughts were now extending with all the power of which they were capable to his uncle, that silent, intent man, whose bald head stretched expansively before him.

Myles Shannon was a singularly fine man, and in thinking of him as such his mind began to fill with imaginations of the man his father must have been. He had never known his father nor, for the matter of that, could he boast of any deep acquaintance with his uncle, yet what an excellent, restrained type of man he was to be sure! Another in the same position as his guardian would have flogged himself into a fury over the mess he had made of his studies.

But it had not been so with his uncle. He had behaved with a calm forbearance. He had supplied him with time and money, and had gone even so far as to look kindly upon the affair with Rebecca Kerr. He had been here since the beginning of the year, and all his uncle had so far said to him by way of asserting his authority was spoken very quietly:

"Now, I'll give you a fair time to think over things. I'll give you till the end of the summer holidays, till after young Brennan comes and goes." These had been his uncle's exact words, and he had not attempted to question them or to qualify them at the time. But just now they were running through his brain with the most curious throbbing insistence. "Till after young Brennan comes and goes." He knew that his uncle had taken an unusual fancy to John Brennan and evidently wished that his summer holidays should be spent enjoyably. But it was a long time until summer, and he was not a person one might conscientiously commend to the friendship of a clerical student. He very often went to Garradrimna.

Ulick had already formed some impressions of his fellow man. He held it as his opinion that at the root of an action, which may appear extraordinary because of its goodness, is always an amount of selfishness. Yet, somehow, as he carefully considered his uncle in the meditative spaces of the breakfast he could not fit him in with this idea.

As he went on with his thought he felt that it was the very excess of his uncle's qualities which had had such a curious effect upon his relations with Rebecca Kerr. It was the very easiness of the path he had afforded to love-making which now made it so difficult. If they had been forbidden and if they had been persecuted, their early affection must have endured more strongly. The opposition of the valley and the village still continued, but Ulick considered their bearing upon him now as he had always considered it—with contempt.

There had been a good deal of wild affection transported into their snatched meetings during the past summer in Donegal. After Christmas, too, he had gone there to see her, and then had happened the climax of their love-making in a quiet cottage within sound of the sea.... Both had moved away from that glowing moment forever changed. Neither could tell of the greatness of the shadow that had fallen between them.

He remembered all her tears on the first evening he had met her after coming back to the valley. There had been nothing in her letters, only the faintest suggestion of some strained feeling. Then had come this unhappy meeting.... She had tortured herself into the belief that it was she who was responsible for his failure.

"With all the time you have wasted coming to see me I have destroyed you. When you should have been at your studies I was taking you up to Donegal."

As he listened to these words between her sobs, there rushed in upon him full realization of all her goodness and the contrast of two pictures her words had called to his mind.... There was he by her side, her head upon his shoulder in that lonely cottage in Donegal, their young lives lighting the cold, bare place around them.... And then the other picture of himself bent low over his dirty, thumb-greased books in that abominable street up and down which a cart was always lumbering. All the torture of this driving him to Doyle's pub at the corner, and afterwards along some squalid street of ill-fame with a few more drunken medical students.

He was glad to be with her again. They met very often during his first month at his uncle's house, in dark spots along the valley road and The Road of the Dead. Then he began to notice a curious reserve springing up between them. She was becoming mysterious while at the same time remaining acutely present in his life.

One morning she had asked him if he intended to remain long in the valley, and he had not known how to reply to her. Another time she had asked him if he was going to retire altogether from the study of medicine, and with what did he intend to occupy himself now? And, upon a certain occasion, she had almost asked him was it the intention of his uncle to leave him the grand farm and the lovely house among the trees?

These were vexatious questions and so different from any part of the talk they used to have here in the valley last summer or at the cottage in Donegal. Her feeling of surrender in his presence had been replaced by a sense of possession which seemed the death of all that kindling of her heart. Then it had happened that, despite the encouragement of his uncle, a shadow had fallen upon his love-affair with Rebecca Kerr.... He was growing tired of his idle existence in the valley. Very slowly he was beginning to see life from a new angle. He was disgusted with himself and with the mess he had made of things in Dublin. He could not say whether it was her talk with him that had shamed him into thinking about it, but he felt again like making something of himself away from this mean place. Once or twice he wondered whether it was because he wanted to get away from her. Somehow his uncle and himself were the only people who seemed directly concerned in the matter. His uncle was a very decent man, and he felt that he could not presume on his hospitality any longer.

Mr. Shannon took off his spectacles and laid by the *Irish Times*. There was an intimate bond between the man and his paper. He always considered it as hitting off his own opinions to a nicety upon any subject under the sun. This always after he had read the leaders which dealt with these subjects. It afforded a contribution to his thought and ideas out of which he spoke with a surer word.

Old Susan Hennessy came into the room with some letters that Farrell McGuinness was after leaving. She hobbled in, a hunched, decrepit woman, now in the concluding stages of her long life as housekeeper to the Shannons, and put the letters into her master's hand.... Then she lingered, quite unnecessarily, about the breakfast-table. Her toothless gums were stripping as words began to struggle into her mouth.... Mr. Shannon took notice of her. This was her usual behavior when she had anything of uncommon interest to say.

"Well, what is it now?" said Mr. Shannon, not without some weariness in his tones, for he expected only to hear some poor piece of local gossip.

"It's how Farrell McGuinness is after telling me, sir, that John Brennan is home."

"Is that a fact?"

"And Farrell says that by the looks on the outside of a certain letter that came to Mrs. Brennan th'other day it is what he is after being expelled."

"Expelled. Well, well!"

There was a mixture of interest and anxiety in Mr. Shannon's tones.

"A good many of those small English colleges are getting broken up and the students drifting into the Army, I suppose that's the reason; but of course they'll say he's been expelled," Ulick ventured as old Susan slipped from the room and down to the loneliness of the kitchen, where she might brood to her heart's content over this glad piece of information, for she was one who well knew the story of John Brennan's mother and "poor Misther Henery Shannon."

"Is that so?" The interest of Mr. Shannon was rapidly mounting towards excitement.

"A case like that is rather hard," said Ulick.

"Yes, it will be rather hard on Mrs. Brennan, I fancy, she being so stuck-up with pride in him."

He could just barely hide his feelings of exultation.

"And John Brennan is not a bad fellow."

"I daresay he's not."

There was now a curious note of impatience in the elder man's tones as if he wished, for some reason or other, to have done speaking of the matter.

"It will probably mean the end of his intention for the Church."

"That is more than likely. These sudden changes have the effect of throwing a shadow over many a young fellow's vocation."

His eyes twinkled, but he fingered his mustache nervously as he said this.

"Funny to think of the two of us getting thrown down together, we being such friends!"

The doubtful humor in the coincidence had appealed to the queer kink that was in the mind of Ulick, and it was because of it he now spoke. It was the merest wantonness that he should have said this thing, and yet it seemed instantly to have struck some hidden chord of deeper thought in his uncle's mind. When Myles Shannon spoke again it was abruptly, and his words seemed to spring out of a sudden impulse:

"You'd better think over that matter of the Army I have just mentioned."

It was the first time his uncle Myles had spoken to him in this way, and now that the rod of correction had fallen even thus lightly he did not like it at all. He felt that his face was already flushing.... And into his mind was burning again the thought of how he had made such a mess of things.... He moved towards the door, and there was his uncle's voice again raised as if in the reproof of authority:

"And where might you be going to-day?"

"Down the valley to see my friend John Brennan, who'll be surely lonely on the first day at home," he said, rather hurriedly, as he went out in the hallway to get his overcoat.

When Myles Shannon was left alone he immediately drifted into deeper thought there in the empty room with his back to the fire. With one hand he clasped his long coat-tails, and with the other nervously twirled his long mustache. He was thinking rapidly, and his thoughts were so strong within him that he was speaking them aloud.

"I might not have gone so far. Don't you see how I might have waited in patience and allowed the hand of Fate to adjust things? See how grandly they are coming around.... And now maybe I have gone too far. Maybe I have helped to spoil Ulick's life into the bargain. And then there's the third party, this girl, Rebecca Kerr?"

He looked straight out before him now, and away over the remains of the breakfast.... He crossed to the window and gazed for a while over the wet fields. He moved into the cold, empty parlor and gazed from its window also over the fields.... Then he turned and for a space remained looking steadfastly at the bureau which held so much of *Her*. Quite suddenly he crossed over and unlocked it.... Yes, there, with the other dead things, were the photograph of Helena Cooper and the letters she had written, and the letter John Brennan's mother had written about him. He raised his eyes from the few, poor relics and they gathered into their depths the loneliness of the parlor.... Here was the picture of this girl, who was young and lovely, while around him, surging emptily forever, was the loneliness of his house. It was Nan Byrne who had driven him to this, and it was Nan Byrne who had ruined his brother Henry.... And yet he was weakly questioning his just feelings of revenge against this woman, but for whom he might now be a happy man. He might have laughter in this house and the sound of children at play. But now he had none of these things, and he was lonely.... He looked into the over-mantel, and there he was, an empty figure, full of a strong family pride that really stood for nothing, a polite survival from the mild romance of the early nineties of the last century, a useless thing amid his flocks and herds. A man who had none of the contentment which comes from the company of a woman or her children, a mean creature, who, during visits to the cattle-market, occasionally wasted his manhood in dingy adventure about low streets in Dublin. One who remained apart from the national thought of his own country reading queer articles in the *Irish Times* about "resolute" government of Ireland.

His head lay low upon his chest because he was a man mightily oppressed by a great feeling of abasement.

"In the desolation of her heart through the destruction of her son," he muttered to himself, not without a certain weariness, as he moved away from the mirror.

CHAPTER XXIV

Whenever a person from the valley went abroad now to fair or market the question was always asked:

"Is it a fact that Ulick Shannon was expelled from the University in Dublin and is at home? And is it a fact that John Brennan is at home from the college he was at too, the grand college in England whose story his mother spread far and wide?"

"That's quite so, ma'am. It's a double fact!"

"Well, well!"

"And is it a fact that they do be always together, going by back ways into the seven publichouses of Garradrimna?"

"Oh, indeed, that's true, ma'am, and now you have the whole of it. Sure it was in the same seven publichouses that the pair of them laid the foundations of their ruination last summer. Sure, do ye know what I'm going to tell you? They couldn't be kept out of them, and that's as sure as you're there!"

Now it was true that if Ulick had gone at all towards Garradrimna it was through very excess of spirits, and it was for the very same reason that he had enticed John Brennan to go with him.... That time they were full of hope and their minds were held by their thoughts of Rebecca. But now, somehow, she seemed to have slipped out of the lives of both of them. And because both had chosen. The feeling had entered into Ulick's heart. But in the case of John Brennan it was not so certain. What had brought him out upon the first morning of his homecoming to take a look at her? It would seem that, through the sudden quickening of his mind towards study just before the break-up of the college, he should have forgotten her.... His life now seemed to hang in the balance shudderingly; a breath might direct it anyway.

He felt that he should have liked to make some suggestions of his own concerning his future, but there was always that tired look of love in his mother's eyes to frustrate his intention.... Often he would go into the sewing-room of a morning and she would say so sadly as she bent over her machine—"I'm contriving, John; I'm contriving!" He had come to the years of manhood and yet he must needs leave every initiative in her hands since she would have it so.... Thus was he driven from the house at many a time of the day.

He went to morning Mass as usual, but the day was long and dreary after that, for the weather was wet and the coldness of winter still lay heavy over the fields. The evenings were the dreariest as he sat over his books in his room and listened to the hum of his mother's machine. Later this would give place to the tumultuous business of his father's home-coming from Garradrimna. Sometimes things were broken, and the noise would destroy his power of application. Thus it was that, for the most part, he avoided the house in the evenings. At the fall of dark he would go slipping along the wet road on his way to Garradrimna. Where the way from Scarden joined the way from Tullahanogue he generally met Ulick Shannon, comfortably top-coated, bound for the same place.

It seemed as if the surrounding power of the talk their presence in the valley had created was driving them towards those scenes in which that talk had pictured them. Through the dusk people would smirk at them as they were seen going the road.... They would slip into McDermott's by the same back way that Ned Brennan had often gone to Brannagan's. Many a time did they pass the place in the woods where John had beheld the adventure of his father and the porter last summer.... In the bottling room of McDermott's they would fancy they were unseen, but Shamesy Golliher or Padna Padna or Thomas James would be always cropping up most unaccountably to tell the tale when they went out into the bar again after what would appear the most accidental glance into the bottling-room.... John would take port wine and Ulick whatever drink he preferred. But even the entertainment of themselves after this fashion did not evoke the subtle spell of last summer. There was no laughter, no stories, even of a questionable kind, when Josie Guinan came to answer their call. Every evening she would ask the question:

"Well, how is Rebecca, Ulick?"

This gross familiarity irritated him greatly, for his decent breeding made him desire that she should keep her distance. Besides he did not want any one to remind him of Rebecca just now. He never answered this question, nor the other by which it was always followed:

"You don't see her very often now, do ye? But of course the woods bees wet these times."

The mere mention of Rebecca's name in this filthy place annoyed John Brennan, who thought of her continuously as some one far beyond all aspects of Garradrimna.

Yet they would be forever coming here to invite this persecution. Ulick would ever and again retreat into long silences that were painful for his companion. But John found some solace come to him through the port wine. So much was this the case that he began to have a certain hankering after spending the evening in this way. When the night had fallen thick and dark over Garradrimna they would come out of McDermott's and spend long hours walking up and down the valley road. Ulick would occasionally give vent to outbursts of talk upon impersonal subjects—the war and politics, the tragic trend of modern literature. John always listened with interest. He never wished to return early to the house, for he dreaded the afflicted drone of his mother reading the holy books to his father by the kitchen fire.

During those brief spells, when the weather brightened for a day or two, he often took walks down by the school and towards the lake.... Always he felt, through power of an oppressive realization, that the eyes of Master Donnellan were upon him as he slipped past the school.... So he began to go by a lane which did not take him before the disappointed eyes of the old man.

Going this way one day he came upon a battered school-reader of an advanced standard, looking so pathetic in its final desertion by its owner, for there is nothing so lonely as the things a schoolboy leaves behind him.... He began to remember the days when he, too, had gone to the valley school and there instituted the great promise which, so far, had not come to fulfilment. He was turning over the leaves when he came on a selection from Carlyle's *French Revolution*—"Thy foot to light on softness, thy eye on splendor." He pondered it as he stood by the water's edge and until it connected itself with his thought of Rebecca. *Thy foot to light on softness, thy eye on splendor.*

It would be nearing three o'clock now, he thought, and Rebecca must soon be going from school. He might see her passing along between the muddy puddles on The Road of the Dead.

He had fallen down before her again.

CHAPTER XXV

In the high, gusty evening Tommy Williams, the gombeen-man, was standing proudly at his own door surveying the street of Garradrimna. It was his custom to appear thus at the close of the day in contemplation of his great possessions. He owned four houses in the village, four proud buildings which advertised his worth before the beggars of the parish—out of whom he had made the price of them. But he was distrustful of his customers to an enormous degree, and his purpose in standing thus at his own door was not altogether one of aimless speculation upon his own spacious importance in Garradrimna. He was watching to see that some people going down the valley road upon ass-carts did not attempt to take away any of the miscellaneous merchandise exhibited outside the door. As he stood against the background of his shop, from which he might be said to have derived his personality, one could view the man in his true proportions beneath his hard, high hat. His short beard was beginning to show tinges of gray, and the deepening look of preoccupation behind his glasses gave him the appearance of becoming daily more and more like John Dillon.

Father O'Keeffe came by and said: "Good-evening, Tommy!" This was a tribute to his respectability and worth. He was the great man of the village, the head and front of everything. Events revolved around him. He would have you know that he was somebody, so he was. A politician after the fashion in the Ireland of his time, he organized and spoke at public meetings. He always wanted to be saying things in support of "The Cause." "The Cause" was to him a kind of poetic ideal. His patriotic imagination had intensified its glory. But it was not the future of Ireland he yearned to see made glorious. He looked forward only to the triumph of "The Cause."

Upon the death of his father, also a patriot, the little mean huckstery at the tail end of the village street had descended to him; and although he had risen to the dignity and proprietorship of four houses, this establishment had never changed, for, among the many ancient superstitions which crowded his mind, the hoary one of the existence of luck where there is muck occupied a place of prominence. And like his father he was a rebel—in his mind. The more notable political mountebanks of his time were all men who had fought as upon a field of battle. Words served them as weapons, and words were the weapons that he loved; he might have died if he were not fighting, and to him talk meant battle. He used to collect all the supplemental pictures of those patriots from *The Weekly Freeman* and paste them in a scrapbook for edification of his eldest son, whom he desired to be some day a unit of their combination. An old-fashioned print of Dan O'Connell hung side by side with a dauby caricature of Robert Emmet in the old porter-smelling parlor off the bar. The names of the two men were linked inseparably with one of his famous phrases—"The undying spirit of Irish Nationality."

Occasionally, when he had a drunken and enthusiastic crowd in that part of his many-sided establishment which was a public bar, he would read out in a fine loud voice how "The Cause" was progressing, and, having learned by heart a speech of John Dillon's, he would lash it out to them as a composition of his own. Whereupon the doubly excited audience would shake his hand as one man and shout: "More power there, mister; 'tis yourself is the true Irishman, me sweet fellow!" He could be very funny too when occasion demanded, and tell stories of Father Healy of Bray at pleasant little dinners which took place in the upper story of his house after every political meeting held in Garradrimna. He never missed the opportunity and the consequent honor of singing "On an old Irish Hill in the Morning" at every one of those dinners. He was always warmly applauded by Father O'Keeffe, who invariably occupied the chair. He was treasurer of the fund, out of which he was paid for supplying all this entertainment.

His wife was the daughter of a farmer of the "red-hat" class. He had been compelled to marry her.... If this had happened to a poor man the talk would have followed him to the grave. But they were afraid to talk censoriously of the patriot who had enveloped all of them. He practically owned them.... The priest could not deliver an attack upon the one who headed his lists of Offerings and Easter Dues and the numerous collections which brought in the decent total of Father O'Keeffe's income.

To Rebecca Kerr had been given the position of governess to the Williams household. She had not sought it, but, on the removal of the two boys, Michael Joseph and Paddy, from the care of Master Donnellan to this more genteel way of imparting knowledge and giving correction, which savored somewhat of the splendor of the Moores of Garradrimna and the Houlihans of Clonabroney, had merely accepted it as part of the system of the place. She had fully anticipated such possibilities upon the very evening of her arrival.... Besides old Master Donnellan had thanked her from his heart for the release she had been the means of affording him, and she liked the master for a quiet, kind old man who did not prate or meddle. So far she had made little improvement in either of the boys. But Mrs. Williams was evidently delighted for "our governess, Miss Kerr," was the one person she ever spoke a good word of to Father O'Keeffe.

This evening Rebecca was in the parlor, seated just beneath the pictures of Dan O'Connell and Robert Emmet, wrestling hard with the boys. All at once her pupils commanded her to be silent. "Whist!" they said in unison. She was momentarily amazed into eavesdropping at their behest....

"Oh, not at all, Mrs. Brennan, sure and I couldn't think of the like at all at all!"

"Well, Mr. Williams, as a well-known benefactor of the college at Ballinamult and a good, religious man to boot, I thought that mebbe you could give John a recommendation. It would be grand to see him there and he working himself up to the summit of his ambition. There would be a great reward to your soul for doing the like of that, Mr. Williams, as sure as you're there."

"And now, woman-a-dear, what about my own sons, Michael Joseph and Paddy?"

"Oh, indeed, there's no fear of them, Mr. Williams!"

"But I could not think of jeopardizing them while I'd be doing for the families or the sons of the stranger."

"But sure, sir, I'll pay you at any rate of interest you like if only you could see your way to give me this help. Enough to buy a bicycle that'll take him over to Ballinamult every day and your grand recommendation to the priests that'll be worth gold. I'll pay you every penny I can, and sure the poor boy will repay you everything when he comes into the position that's due to him."

"Well, I don't know. I don't think the missus—"

At this very moment Mrs. Williams came into the parlor where Rebecca sat with them, and beamed upon her sons.

"Oh, my poor boys, sure it is killed you are with the terrible strain of the study. Sure it is what you'd better go out into the fields now with the pony; but mind, be careful! You poor little fellows!"

Michael Joseph and Paddy at once snatched up their caps and rushed for the door. So much for the extent of their training and Rebecca's control of them, for this was a daily happening. But another part of her hour of torture at the gombeen-man's house had yet to come. Of late Mrs. Williams had made of her a kind of *confidante* in the small concerns of her household. She was the sort of woman who must needs be always talking to some one of her affairs. Now she enlarged upon the immediate story of how Mrs. Brennan had been begging and craving of Tommy to do something for her son John, who had been sent home from the place he was in England. "The cheek of her, mind you, that Mrs. Brennan!" emphasized Mrs. Williams.

If it had been any other schoolmistress or girl of any kind at all that Mrs. Williams had ever known, they would have acquiesced in this statement of denunciation and said: "That's a sure fact for you, ma'am!" or "Just so!" But this had never been Rebecca's way. She merely said: "John Brennan is a very nice young fellow!"

Although Mrs. Williams was surprised, she merely said: "Is that so? Sure I know very little about him only to see him pass the door. They say he's taken the fashion of tippling a bit, and it's to McDermott's he does go, d'ye mind, with Ulick Shannon, and not to this house. But, of course, it's my bold Ulick that's spending. Easy for him, begad, and it not his own."

Rebecca saw the dirty meanness that stirred in this speech.

"That's what they say and it is surely a great pity to see him wasting his time about the roads of the valley. I think it would be a grand piece of charity on the part of any one who would be the means of taking him away from this place. If only he could be afforded some little help. 'Tis surely not his fault that the college in England broke down, and although his mother is, I believe, contriving the best for his future, sure it is hard for her. She is only a poor woman, and the people of the valley seem queerly set against her. I don't know why. They seem to hate the very sight of her."

"You may say that indeed, and it is the good reasons they have—"

Mrs. Williams suddenly checked herself, for there flashed across her mind a chapter of her own story. She had been one of the lucky ones.... Besides, by slow steps, Rebecca was coming to have some power over her.

"Of course it would be no loss to Tommy if he did give this help. He'd be bound to get the interest of his money, even if he were to sell her out of house and home. He knows his business, and he's not against it himself, I may tell you; for he sees a return in many a way. It was myself that was keeping him from it on account of the boy's mother. But, of course, if you think it would be a nice, good thing to do—"

"It would be a good thing, and a very good thing, and one of the best actions you could put for luck before your own sons."

"Oh, indeed, there's no fear of them! Is it Michael Joseph or Paddy?"

"Of course not, indeed, nor did I mean anything of the kind. I only said it to soften you, Mrs. Williams."

"Well, I may tell you it's all right, Miss Kerr. Mrs. Brennan is out there in the shop, and she's craving from me man.... It'll be all right, Miss Kerr, and that's a fact.... I'll make it all right, never you fear!"

In this way was John Brennan again led back into the paths of the Church. Curious that it should have been given Rebecca to effect the change in his condition—Rebecca, whose beauty, snatching at his spirit always, had drawn his mind into other ways of contemplation. In less than a week, through the powerful ecclesiastical influence of Tommy Williams, the gombeen-man, he was riding daily to the college at Ballinamult. By teaching outside the hours allotted for his own study he was earning part of his fees, and, as a further example of his worth to the community, Tommy Williams was paying the other portion, although as a purely financial speculation.... In a year it was expected he would win one of the Diocesan Scholarships and go up to Maynooth. Mrs. Brennan knew more joy than had ever before possessed her. Her son was to be ordained in Ireland after all, and maybe given a curacy in his own diocese. Who knew but he might yet follow in the footsteps of Father O'Keeffe and become Parish Priest of Garradrimna while she was still alive here in this little house in the valley!

CHAPTER XXVI

The meetings of Ulick and Rebecca had become less and less frequent. Sometimes she would not see him for days at a stretch, and such periods would appear as desert spaces. She would be driven by them into the life of the valley, where no echo of comfort ever came to her. Even the little children created an irritation with their bright faces continually reminding her of all the prayers they had said for her intentions.... It was curious that she never asked them to say a prayer for her intentions now. And their looks would seem to be beseeching her forever. And yet she could not—she could not ask them now.... Each distinct phase of the day seemed to hold for her its own peculiar tortures. These seemed to have reached their climax and very moment of ecstasy on the days succeeding upon one another when Monica McKeon came in at the recreation hour to take her luncheon in company with Mrs. Wyse.

Monica would be certain to say with the most unfailing regularity and, in fact, with exactly the same intonation upon all occasions: "I wonder when that Ulick Shannon is going away?" To which Mrs. Wyse would reply in a tone which would seem to have comprehended all knowledge: "Ah, sure, he'll never go far!" Presently Monica would begin to let fall from her slyly her usual string of phrases: "Wouldn't you be inclined to say, now, that Ulick Shannon is good-looking?" Talking of some other one, she would describe him as being "Just like Ulick Shannon, don't you know!" And if they happened to be discussing the passage of some small event it would invariably circle around the breathless point of interest—"And who do you think was there only Ulick Shannon?" Then from where she sat supping her tea out of a saucerless cup Mrs. Wyse would give out her full opinion of Ulick Shannon.

"He's the quare sort, just like his father. I don't think I've ever seen a son to take after his father so closely. And *he* was what you might call a quare character in his day. It was said that a girl as well as lost her good name if she was seen talking twice in succession to Henry Shannon, he was that bad. Like father, like son is surely the case between Henry and Ulick Shannon!"

This seemed at all times the strangest talk for Rebecca to be hearing.... It often caused her to shiver even though spring was well on its way. And they would never let it out of their minds; they would never let it rest. They were always talking at her about Ulick Shannon, for they seemed to know.

But no one knew save herself. It was a grand secret. Not even Ulick knew. She hugged the dear possession of her knowledge to herself. There was the strangest excitement upon her to escape from school in the evenings so that she might enjoy her secret in loneliness.

Even this joy had been dissipated by her certainty of meeting John Brennan somewhere upon the road in the near vicinity of the school.... Now, as she thought of it upon an evening a few days after she had spoken to Mrs. Williams in his favor, she fancied that his lonely admiration for her must have been growing in strength since his return.... There had always been a sense of sudden relief in his presence after the torture of the two women, a feeling of high emancipation like the rushing in of some clean wind.... Only a few words had ever passed between them on those occasions, but now they were to her throbbing brain of blessed and sweet memory. And there had always been the same look upon his face, making her try to puzzle out in what possible way he could look upon her. Could it be in the way she had looked upon him, with a full kindliness working into the most marvelous ways of sympathy? Yet she missed him ever so much, now that he was to be no longer seen upon the road.

It was strange enough, too, as she thought of it, that although the reason of Mrs. Williams in taking a fancy to her was no more than the selfish one of showing her dislike for Master Donnellan, it should have borne good fruit after this fashion. Yet a certain loneliness, a certain feeling of empty sadness was to be her reward because she had done a good thing.... No one at all now to take her mind away as she wandered from torture to torture in the afternoons.... On one of the first evenings of the changed condition of things Mrs. McGoldrick, noticing in her keen mind that Rebecca was a minute or so earlier than usual, said, after the manner of one proud of being able to say it:

"Is it a fact, Miss Kerr, that John Brennan bees going as a kind of a charity teacher or something to the college at Ballinamult?"

"Well, if it's a fact, it is a fact," said Rebecca in a tired, dull voice and without showing any interest whatsoever. But even this attitude did not baulk the sergeant's wife, for she hurried on:

"Ah, God help his innocent wit, but sure he'll never be a priest, he'll never be a priest! 'Tis a pity of his mother, but sure she could hardly expect it to be so, for she wasn't a good woman, they tell me, and she ought to know, you know, that she could hardly expect it to be so!"

Rebecca saw at once that her landlady was in one of her fits of garrulousness, so she concluded in consequence that there would not be much pleasure in her dinner to-day. She passed it untasted and went upstairs wearily. There was a certain grim comfort in thinking that she had left Mrs. McGoldrick with her harangue unfinished and a great longing upon her to be talking.... She flung herself upon the bed in the still untidied room. She was weary with some great, immeasurable weariness this blessed evening.... Her corset hurt her, and she sat up again to take it off. She caught sight of herself reflected in the mirror opposite.... How worn she looked! Her brows, with their even curves, did not take from the desolation that had fallen upon her forehead, where it was grown harder as beneath the blows of some tyrannic thought. And it seemed as if the same thought had plowed all the lines which were beginning to appear there now.... It must be that she had long since entered into a mood of mourning for the things she had lost in the valley.

She fell to remembering the first evening she had come to it, and of how she had begun to play with her beauty on that very first evening. It had appeared then as the only toy in her possession in this place of dreary immensity. And now it seemed to have run through many and sudden vicissitudes. She had allowed Ulick Shannon to play with it too.... But his language had been so sweet when he had praised her in the silent woods.... And in the lonely cottage in Donegal, where he had gone to see her after Christmas, there had been abiding joy, while outside the night swept wild and dark upon the cold, gray sea.... Here there came sudden qualms as to whether she had helped to ruin him by taking him away from preparation for his final exam. But there was such an urge of dear remembrance upon her that her mind sprang quickly back again to all the thoughts they had had between them then.... Back into her mind too were thronging the exact words he had used upon that night they had spent together in the cottage.

And by the side of all this, was it not queer that he came so seldom to see her now although he lived distant from her by only a few fields? Even when he came their partings were so abrupt, after a little period of strained conversation, when he always went with a slight excuse in his mouth to Garradrimna. Yet all the time she longed for his presence by her side with an even greater longing than that she had experienced in Donegal.... It was also painfully notable how he gave shifty answers to her every question. And had she not a good right to be asking him questions now?... And surely he must guess by this time.

She threw her head back upon the pillow once more, and once more she was weeping. She thought, through the mist of her tears, of how she had so bitterly wept upon the first evening of her coming to this room. But on that evening also she had prayed, and she could not pray now. Nor could she sleep. She remained there upon the bed, inert in every sense save for her empty stare up at the discolored ceiling. It was broken only by the queer smile she would take to herself ever and again.... At last she began to count upon her fingers. She was simply counting the number of times she had seen Ulick since his return to his uncle's house.

"Oh, dear, dear, and what have I done to him?" she muttered incessantly, biting her lips occasionally between her words as if in a very ecstasy of desire for the pain he was causing her.... There came moments, winged and clean like shining angels, to bring her comfort, when she wildly fancied it was the very loveliest thing to endure great pain for his sake.

But the powers of her mind for any wild gladness were being gradually annihilated by dark thoughts coming down to defeat her thoughts of beauty. She turned from contemplation of the ceiling and began to glance around the room in search of some distraction. In one corner she saw an old novelette thrown aside in its gaudy covers. The reading of rubbish was Mrs. McGoldrick's recreation when she was not sewing or nursing the baby.

She had called the girls after heroines of passionate love-stories, just as her husband, the sergeant, had seen that the boys were called after famous men in the world of the police. Thus the girls bore names like Euphemia McGoldrick and Clementina McGoldrick, while the boys bore names like John Ross McGoldrick and Neville Chamberlain McGoldrick. The girls, although they were ugly and ill-mannered, had already been invested with the golden lure of Romance, and the boys were already policemen although they were still far distant from the age when they could put on a belt or a baton.

Rebecca began to snatch at paragraphs here and there through the story, which was entitled *The Desecration of the Hearth*. There was one passage which seemed to hold an unaccountable fascination as her eyes lingered over it:

> "*Then suddenly, and without a minute's warning, Lord Archibald Molyneux dashed the poor, ruined girl from him, and soon she was struggling for life in the swirling stream.*
>
> "*'Ah-a-ha!' he said once more, hissing out his every word between his thin, cruel lips. 'That will may be put an end to your scandalous allegations against a scion of the noble house of Molyneux.'*
>
> "*'Mercy! Pity! Oh, God! The Child!' she wailed piteously as she felt herself being caught in the maelstrom of the current.*
>
> "*But Lord Archibald Molyneux merely twirled his dark, handsome mustache with his white hands, after the fashion that was peculiar to him, and waited until his unfortunate victim had disappeared completely beneath the surface of the water.*"

Rebecca's eyes had closed over the passage, and she was dozing now, but only fitfully.... To occupy small instants would come the most terrifying dreams in long waves of horror which would seem to take great spaces of time for their final passage from her mind. Then there would flow in a brief space of respite, but only as a prelude to the dread recurrence of her dreams again. And all jumbled together, bits of wild reality which were and were not parts of her experience would cause her to start up ever and anon.

There fell a knock upon the door, and a little girl came in with some tea-things on a tray. She called: "Miss Kerr, your tea!" and when Rebecca woke up with a terrible start it appeared as if she had not slumbered at all.

"Oh, is that yourself, Euphemia? I declare to goodness the dusk is falling outside. I must have been sleeping."

"Yes, miss!"

"You are late in coming this evening?"

"Well, wait till I tell you, miss. I went into the village for some things for my mother, and what d'ye think but when I was coming home I thought I saw a strange man just outside the ditch opposite the door, and I was afraid for to pass, so I was."

"A strange man! Is that a fact?"

"Well, sure then I thought, miss, it might be Ulick Shannon, but I may tell you I got the surprise of my life when I found it was only John Brennan, and he standing there alone by himself looking up at your window."

Long before she had got through it, with many lisps and lapses, Rebecca was wearied by the triteness of the little one's statement, so well copied was it from the model of her mother's gossipy communication of the simplest fact.

But what could John Brennan be doing there so near her again? This was the thought that held Rebecca as she went on with an attempt to take her tea.

CHAPTER XXVII

John Brennan came down the valley. The trees by the roadside were being shaken heavily by soft winds. Yet, for all the kindness of May that lingered about it, there seemed to be some shadow hanging over the evening. No look of peace or pity had struggled into the squinting windows.... Would the valley ever again put on the smile it had worn last summer? That time it had been so dearly magnified. At leaving it there had been such a crush of feeling in his breast.

He seemed to see it more clearly now. There was something that hurt him in the thought of how he was preparing for a genteel kind of life while his father remained a common sponger around the seven publichouses of Garradrimna, asking people to stand him drinks for the love of God like Anthony Shaughness. He could not forget that the valley had wrought this destruction upon Ned Brennan, and that Ned Brennan was his father.

This thought arose out of a definite cause. At the college in Ballinamult he had made the acquaintance of Father George Considine, who had already begun to exercise an influence over him. This priest was a simple, holy man, who had devoted his life usefully, remaining far away from the ways of pride. Although gombeen-men like Tommy Williams had some influence with those who controlled the college, they had no influence over him. He was in curious contrast to the system which tied him to this place. It was impossible to think that his ordination had represented a triumph to any one at all, yet he had been far ahead of his contemporaries and while yet a young man had been made principal of this college in Ballinamult. His name had gone out into the world. The satisfaction that had been denied to Master Donnellan was his. He had had a hand in the education of men whose names were now notable in many a walk of life. And yet, to see him moving about the grounds of the college in his faded coat with the frayed sleeves and shiny collar, no man would think that his name, the name of "poor Father Considine," was spoken with respect in distant places.

But Mrs. Brennan did not approve of him. On the evening of John's first day in Ballinamult, after she had made every other possible inquiry she said:

"And did you meet Father Considine?"

"I did indeed, mother; a nice man!"

"Ah, a quare ould oddity! Wouldn't you think now that he'd have a little pride in himself and dress a bit better, and he such a very learned man?"

"Maybe that's just the reason why he's not proud. The saints were not proud, mother; then why should he be?"

She always gave a deaf ear to any word of this kind from John, for her ideal was Father O'Keeffe, with his patent leather top-boots, silver-mounted whip and silk hat, riding to hounds with the Cromwellian descendants of the district.... Here was where Father Considine stood out in sharp contrast, for he was in spiritual descent from those priests who had died with the people in the Penal Days. It was men like him who had carried down the grandeur of Faith and Idealism from generation to generation. One felt that life was a small thing to him beyond the chance it gave to make it beautiful. He had written a little book of poems in honor of Mary, the Mother of God, and to feel that it had brought some comfort to many a troubled one and to know that he had been the means of shaping young men's lives towards useful ends was all that this world meant to him.

John Brennan knew very well that if he became a priest it was in the steps of Father Considine he would follow rather than in those of Father O'Keeffe. This he felt must mean the frustration of half his mother's grand desire, but, inevitable, it must be so, for it was the way his meditative mind would lead him. Thus was he troubled again.

Father Considine had spoken to him of Father O'Keeffe:

"A touch of the farmer about that man don't you think? But maybe a worthy man for all that!"

Then he had looked long into the young man's eyes and said:

"Be humble, my son, be humble, so that great things may be done unto you!"

John had pondered these words as he cycled home that evening past the rich fields. He began to think how his friend Ulick would have put all his thoughts so clearly. How he would have spoken of the rank green grass now rising high over County Meath as a growth that had sprung from the graves of men's rotted souls; of all the hate and pride that had come out of their hunger for the luscious land; of how Faith and Love and Beauty had gone forever from this golden vale to the wild places of his country, where there was a letting-in of wind and sun and sea.... It was easy to connect Father O'Keeffe's pride with the land. Remembrance of the man's appearance was sufficient. It was not so easy in the case of his mother. But, of course, John had no knowledge of how she had set her heart upon Henry Shannon's lovely farm in the days gone by.

Hitherto his thoughts of his future condition had been bound up with consideration of his mother, but now there had come this realization of his father. It was not without its sadness to think that his father had been a stranger to him always and that he should now behold him stumbling down to old age amid the degradation of Garradrimna. He felt curiously desirous of doing something for him. But the heavy constraint between them still existed as always. He was unequal to the task of plucking up courage to speak to him. This evening, too, as he tried, after his accustomed fashion, in a vacant moment to catch a glimpse of his own future, he acutely felt the impossibility of seeing himself as a monument of pride.... Always there would arise before his mind a broken column in the middle of the valley.

And he was lonely. He had not seen Ulick Shannon or Rebecca since he had begun to cycle daily to Ballinamult. Often, in some of the vacant stretches of thought which came to him as he hurried along, he pictured the two of them meeting during some of those long, sweet evenings and being kind to one another. Despite sudden flashes of a different regard that would come sweeping his thoughts of all kinds, he loved these two and was glad that they were fond of one another. It now seemed surprising that he had ever thought so deeply of Rebecca Kerr, and wished to meet her upon the road and look longingly into her eyes. All this while going on to be a priest seemed far from him now that he had begun to be influenced by Father Considine.

He had to pass the house of Sergeant McGoldrick by the way he was going, and it seemed an action altogether outside him that he had gone into an adjacent field and gazed for quite a long time up at her window.... He was all confusion when he noticed the child of the McGoldricks observing him.... He drifted away, his cheeks hot and a little sense of shame dimming his eyes.... He took to the road again and at once saw Ulick Shannon coming towards him. The old, insinuating smile which had so often been used upon his weak points, was spread over the face of his friend.

"And at last you have succeeded in coming to see her thus far?"

The words seemed to fall out of Ulick's oblique smile.

"She?" he said in surprise.

"Oh, I thought it was that you had intentions of becoming my rival!"

John laughed now, for this was the old Ulick come back again. He went on laughing as if at a good joke, and the two students went together down the road.

"Don't let me delay you!" John said abruptly.

"Oh, you're not preventing me in any way at all."

"But Rebecca?"

"Even the austerities of Ballinamult have not made you forget Rebecca?"

"Hardly—I shouldn't like to think that I had been the cause of keeping you from her even for a short while."

There came between them now one of those long spells of silence which seemed essential parts of their friendship.

"You're in a queer mood this evening?" John said at last.

"I suppose I am, and that there's no use in trying to hide it.... D'ye know what it is, Brennan? We two seem to have changed a great deal since last summer. *I* simply can't look at things in the same light-hearted way. I suppose I went too far, and that I must be paying for it now. But there are just a few things I have done for which I am sorry—I'm sorry about this affair with Rebecca Kerr."

John was listening with quiet attention to the remarks which Ulick was letting fall from him disjointedly.

"I'm sorry, sorry, sorry that I should ever have come here to meet her, for somehow it has brought me to this state of mind and not to any happiness at all. I'm doubtful, too, if it has brought any happiness to her."

"That's strange," said John, "and I thought you two were very happy in your friendship."

"Happiness!" jerked out the other in a full, strong sneer. "That's a funny word now, and a funny thing. Do you think that we deserve happiness any more than those we see working around us in the valley? Not at all! Rather less do we deserve. Just think of them giving their blood and sweat so crudely in mortal combat with the fields! And what does it avail them in the end? What do they get out of it but the satisfaction of a few unkind thoughts and a few low lies? In the mean living of their own lives they represent futile expeditions in quest of joy. Yet what brings the greatest joy it is possible for them to experience? Why, the fact that another's hope of happiness has been finally desolated. If any great disaster should suddenly come upon one or other of the three of us, upon you or me or Rebecca Kerr, they would see more glory in the fulfilment of their spite than in the harvest promise of their fields. And yet I here assert that these deserve to be happy. They labor in the hard way it was ordained that man should labor at Adam's fall, and they attend to their religion. They pray for happiness, and this is the happiness that comes to them. Some must be defeated and driven down from the hills of their dreams so that the other ones, the deserving and the pious, may be given material for their reward of joy. That, Brennan, is the only happiness that ever descends upon the people of the valley. It may be said that they get their reward in this life."

Ulick was in one of those moods of eloquence which always came to him after a visit to Garradrimna, and when a very torrent of words might be expected to pour forth from him. John Brennan merely lifted his eyebrows in mild surprise and said nothing as the other went on:

"Happiness indeed. What have I ever done to deserve happiness? I have not worked like a horse, I have not prayed?"

"I was not thinking of any broad generalizations of happiness. I was only thinking of happiness in your relation to Rebecca Kerr."

Ulick now gave a sudden turn to the conversation:

"Where were you wandering to the night?" he inquired of John Brennan.

"Oh, nowhere in particular—just down the road."

"Well, it seems strange that you should have come this way, past the house of Sergeant McGoldrick."

It appeared as if Ulick had glimpsed the tender spot upon which John Brennan's thoughts were working and struck it with the sharp point of his words. John did not reply, but it could be seen that his cheeks were blushing even in the gloom that had come towards them down the road.

"I hope you will be very kind to her, John, when I am gone from here. She's very nice, and this is the drear, lonely place for her to be. I expect to be going away pretty soon."

It seemed extraordinary that this thing should be happening now.... He began to remember how he had longed for Rebecca last summer, and how his poor yearning had been reduced to nothing by the favor with which she looked upon his friend. And later how he had turned away out of the full goodness of his own heart and returned again through power of a fateful accident to his early purpose. And now how the good influence of Father Considine had just come into his life to lead him finally into the way for which he had been intended by his mother from the beginning.

He did not yet fully realize that this quiet and casual meeting which had been effected because Ulick Shannon had accidentally come around this way from Garradrimna represented the little moment which stood for the turning-point of his life. But it had certainly moved into being along definite lines of dramatic significance.

Presently Ulick mounted a stile which gave upon a path leading up through the fields of his uncle Myles and to the lonely house among the trees. Then it was true that he was not seeing Rebecca to-night.... A great gladness seemed to have rushed in upon John Brennan because he had become aware of this thing. And further, Ulick Shannon was going away from the valley and Rebecca remaining here to be lonely. But he, who had once so dearly longed for her company, would be coming and going from the valley daily, and summer was upon them again.... Ulick must have bade him a "Good-night!" that he had not heard, for already he could see him disappearing into the sea of white mist which would seem to have rolled into the valley from the eternity of the silent places.... He was left here now upon this lonely, quiet shore while his mind had turned into a tumbling sea.

When at last he roused himself and went into the kitchen he saw that his mother had already settled herself to the task of reading a religious paper to his father.... The elder man was sitting there so woebegone by the few wet sods that were the fire. He was not very drunk this evening, and the usual wild glint in his eyes was replaced by the look of one who is having thoughts of final dissolution.... John experienced a little shudder with the thought that he did not possess any desire to speak to his father now.

But his mother had broken in with a question:

"Was that Ulick Shannon was with you outside just now?"

"Yes, mother, it was."

"He went home very early, didn't he?"

"I suppose it is rather early for him to go home."

"I think 'tis very seldom he bees with Rebecca Kerr now, whatever's the reason, *whatever's the reason.*"

It was her repetition and emphasis of the final words which brought about the outburst.

Ned Brennan suddenly flamed up and snarled out:

"Look ye here, Nan Byrne, that's no kind of talk to be giving out to your grand, fine, educated young fellow of a son, and he be going on to be a priest. That's the quare, suggestive kind of talk. But sure 'tis very like you, Nan Byrne. 'Tis very like you!"

Mrs. Brennan had just been on the point of beginning to read the religious paper, and, with the thought of all her reading surging in upon her in one crushing moment, she felt the cutting rebuff most keenly and showed her confusion. She made no reply as John went up to the room where his books were.... Long after, as he tried to recall forgotten, peaceful thoughts, he could hear his father speaking out of the heat of anger in the kitchen below.

CHAPTER XXVIII

After she had failed to take her tea Rebecca walked the valley road many times, passing and repassing their usual meeting place. But no sign of Ulick did she find. She peered longingly into the sea of white fog, but he did not come.... What in the world was happening to him at all? Never before had he missed this night of the week.... She did not care to return so early, for she feared that Mrs. McGoldrick might come with that awful look of scrutiny she detested. Just to pass the time she wandered down The Road of the Dead towards the lake. To-night it seemed so lonely set there amid the sea of white.

It was strange to think that this place could ever have had a fair look about it or given pleasure to any person at all. Yet it was here that John Brennan had loved to walk and dream. She wondered how it was with him now. She began to think of the liking he had shown for her. Maybe he fancied she did not know why he happened to meet her so often upon the road. But well did she know—well. And to think that he had come to look up at her window this evening.

Yet even now she was fearful of acknowledging these things to herself. It appeared as a double sacrilege. It was an attack upon her love for Ulick and it questioned the noble intention of Mrs. Brennan in devoting her son to God. But all chance that it might ever come to anything was now over. The ending had been effected by herself in the parlor of Tommy Williams, the gombeen-man, and Mrs. Brennan might never be able to guess the hand she had had in it. It was a thing upon which she might well pride herself if there grew in her the roots of pride. But she was not of that sort. And now she was in no frame of delight at all for the thought of him had united her unto the thought of Ulick, and Ulick had not come to her this evening.... She felt herself growing cold in the enveloping mist. The fir trees were like tall ghosts in the surrounding gloom.... But immediately the lake had lost its aspect of terror when she remembered what she had done might have averted the possibility of having John Brennan ever again to wander lonely.... And yes, in spite of any comforting thought, the place would continue to fill her with a nameless dread. She was shivering and expectant.

Suddenly a big pike made a splash among the reeds and Rebecca gave a loud, wild cry. It rang all down the lonely aisle of the fir-trees and united its sound with that of a lone bird crying on the other side of the lake. Then it died upon the banks of mist up against the silent hills.

For a few moments its source seemed to flutter and bubble within her breast, and then it ended in a long, sobbing question to herself—Why had she cried out at all? She might have known it was only a fish or some such harmless thing. And any one within reasonable distance could have heard the cry and thought it was the signal of some terrible thing that had happened here by the lakeside. It was not so far distant from two roads, and who knew but some one had heard? Yet she could hardly fancy herself behaving in this way if she had not possessed an idea that it was a lonely place and seldom that any one went by in the night-time.

But she hurried away from the feeling of terror she had caused to fill the place and back towards the house of Sergeant McGoldrick. As quickly as possible she got to bed. Here seemed a little comfort. She remembered how this had been her place of refuge as a child, how she felt safe from all ghosts and goblins once her head was hidden beneath the clothes. And the instinct had survived into womanhood.

Again a series of those fitful, half sleeping and waking conditions began to pass over her. Side by side with the most dreadful feelings of impending doom came thronging memories of glad phases of life through which she had passed.... And to think that this life of hers was now narrowing towards this end. Were the valley and its people to behold her final disaster? Was it to be that way with her?

She had intended to tell Ulick if he had come to her this evening, but he had not come, and what was she to do now? In the slough of her torment she could not think of the right thing.... Maybe if she wrote an angry letter upbraiding him.... But how could she write an angry letter to him? Yet she must let him know, and immediately—when the dawn had broken into the room she would write. For there was no use in thinking of sleeping. She could not sleep. Yes, when the dawn had broken into the room she would write surely. But not an angry letter.... Very slowly she began to notice the corners of the room appearing in the new light before her wide open eyes. And to feel that this was the place she had so fiercely hated from the first moment of setting foot in it, and that it was now about to see her write the acknowledgment of her shame.... The dawn was a great while in breaking.... If he did not—well then, what could her future life hope to be? She began to grow strangely dizzy as she fell to thinking of it. Dizzy and fearful as she drew near in mind to that very great abyss.

The leaping-up of the day did not fill her with any of its gradual delight.... She rose with a weariness numbing her limbs. The putting-on of her few clothes was an immense task.... She went to the table upon which she had written all those letters to her school-companions which described that "there was nothing like a girlfriend." She pulled towards her, with a small, trembling hand, the box of *Ancient Irish Vellum*, upon which her special letters were always written. Her mind had focussed itself to such small compass that this letter seemed more important than any that had ever before been written in this world.

But for a long time she could not begin. She did not know by what term of endearment to address him now.... They had been so particularly intimate.... And then it was so hard to describe her condition to him in poor words of writing with pen and ink upon paper. If only he had come to her last night it might have been a task of far less difficulty. A few sobs, a gathering of her little troubled body unto him, and a beseeching look up into his face.... But it was so hard to put any single feeling into any separate sentence.

After hours, during which the sun had been mounting high and bright, she had the letter finished at last and was reading it over. Some sentences like the following leaped out before her eyes here within this sickly-looking room— Whatever was the matter with him that he could not come to her? Surely he was not so blind, and he with his medical knowledge. He must know what was the matter with her, and that this was scarcely the time to be leaving her alone. His uncle, Myles Shannon, was a very rich man, and did he not remember how often he had told her how his uncle looked with favor upon her? Here she included the very words in which Ulick had many a time described his uncle's opinion of her—"I like that little schoolmistress, Rebecca Kerr!" "It was all so grand, Ulick, our love and meetings; but here comes the paying of the penalty, and surely you will not leave poor little me to pay it in full. You have enjoyed me, have you not, Ulick?" She was more immediately personal now, and this was exactly how the sentences continued: "You know very well what this will mean to me. I'll have to go away from here, and where, I ask you, can I go? Not back to my father's house surely, nor to my aunt's little cottage in Donegal.... I have no money. The poor salary I earn here is barely able to buy me a little food and clothing and keep a roof over my head. Did I not often tell you that when you were away from me there were times when I could hardly afford the price of stamps? If it should happen that this thing become public while I am yet here I could never get another day's teaching, for Father O'Keeffe would warn every manager in Ireland against engaging me. But surely, darling, you will not allow things to go so far.... You will please come down to see me at 5.30 this evening. You will find me at the old place upon The Road of the Dead. Don't you remember that it was there we had our first talk, Ulick?"

Great as the torture of writing it had been, the torture of reading it was still greater. Some of the lines seemed to lash out and strike her and to fill her eyes with tears, and there were some that seemed so hard upon him that she struck them out, not wishing, as ever, to hurt her dearest Ulick at all. At one moment she felt a curious desire to tear it into pieces and let her fate come to her as it had been ordained from the beginning.... But there was little Euphemia McGoldrick knocking at the door to be allowed to enter with the breakfast. Who would ever imagine that it was so late?

She had written a great deal. Why it filled pages and pages. She hurriedly thrust it into a large envelope that she had bought for the purpose of sending a card of greeting to John Brennan at Christmas, thinking better of it only at the last moment. It was useful now, for the many sheets were bulky.

"The breakfast, miss!" announced Euphemia as she left the room.

This was the third meal in twenty-four hours that Rebecca could make no attempt to take, but, to avert suspicion, she wrapped up the sliced and buttered bread in a few leaves from the novelette from which she had read those desperate passages on the previous evening. The tea she threw out into the garden. It fell in a shining shower down over the bright green vegetables.... She put on her dust-coat and, stuffing the letter to Ulick into one pocket and her uneaten breakfast by way of a luncheon she would not eat into the other, hurried out of doors and up the road, for this morning she had important business in the village before going on to the school.

Mrs. McGoldrick was set near the foot of the stairs holding Euphemia and Clementina by the hand, all three in action there to behold the exit of Rebecca. This was a morning custom and something in the nature of a rite. It was the last clout of torture always inflicted by Mrs. McGoldrick.

Rebecca went on into Garradrimna. The village street was deserted save by Thomas James, who held solitary occupation. He was posting the bills for a circus at the market square. She was excited as she went over to speak to him and did not notice the eyes of the bespectacled postmistress that were trained upon her from the office window with the relentlessness of howitzers. She asked Thomas James would he take a letter from her to Mr. Ulick Shannon.

"Oh yes, miss; O Lord, yes!"

She slipped the letter into his hand when she thought that no one was looking. She had adopted this mode of caution in preference to sending it through the Post Office. She was evidently anxious that it should be delivered quickly and unread by any other person.

"O Lord, yes, miss; just as soon as I have an auction bill posted after this. You know, miss, that Mickeen Connellan, the auctioneer, is one of my best patrons. He doesn't pay as well as the circus people, but he pays oftener."

That was in the nature of a very broad hint, but Rebecca had anticipated it and had the shilling already prepared and ready to slip into his other hand.

"Thanks, miss!"

With remarkable alacrity Thomas James had "downed tools" and disappeared into Brannagan's. Rebecca could hear the swish of his pint as she went by the door after having remained a few moments looking at the lurid circus-bills. Inside, Mrs. Brannagan, the publican and victualler's wife, took notice that he possessed the air of a man bent upon business.

"Ah, it's how I'm going to do a little message for the assistant schoolmistress," he said, taking his matutinal pinch of salt, for this was his first pint and one could never tell what might happen.

"Is that so?"

"Aye, indeed; a letter to young Shannon."

"Well now? And why for wouldn't it do to send it by the post?"

"Ah, mebbe that way wouldn't be grand enough for her. Mebbe it is what it would be too chape—a penny, you know, for the stamp, and this costs a shilling for the porter. Give us another volume of this, Mrs. Brannagan, if you please? Ha-ha-ha!" He laughed loudly, but without any mirth, at his own joke and the peculiar blend of subtlety by which he had marked it.

Mrs. Brannagan was all anxiety and excitement about the letter.

"Well now, just imagine!" she said to herself about forty times as she filled the second pint for Thomas James. Then she rose up from her bent posture at the half barrel and, placing the drink before him on the bar, said:

"I wonder what would be in that letter. Let me see?"

"Oh, 'tis only a letter in a big envelope. Aren't you the inquisitive woman now, Mrs. Brannagan?"

"What'll you have, Thomas?"

"Ah, another pint, Mrs. Brannagan, thanks!"

His second drink had been despatched with his own celebrated speed.

Mrs. Brannagan was a notably hard woman, and he could not let the opportunity of having her stand him a drink go by. She was the hardest woman in Garradrimna. Her childlessness had made her so. She was beginning to grow stale and withered, and anything in the nature of love and marriage, with their possible results, was to her a constant source of affliction and annoyance.

Her heart was now bounding within her breast in curiosity.

"Drink that quick, Thomas, and have another before the boss comes down." But there was no need to command him. It had already disappeared.... The fourth pint had found its way to his lips. He was beginning to grow mellow now and to lose his cross-sickness of the morning.

"Will ye let me see the letter?"

"Certainly, Mrs. Brannagan. O Lord, yes!"

He handed it across the counter.

"Such a quare letter? Oh, I hear the boss coming in across the yard." ... She had taken the empty glass from before Thomas James, and again was it filled.... Her husband stood before her. And this was the moment she had worked up to so well.

"I'll hand it back to you when he goes out," she whispered.

"All right, ma'am!"

Thomas James and Mr. Brannagan fell into a chat while she went towards the kitchen. She took the letter from her flat bosom, where she had hastily thrust it and looked at it from every possible angle. It seemed to possess a compelling attraction. But she could not open it here. She would run across to her friend the postmistress, who had every appliance for an operation of the kind. Besides she was the person who had first right to open it.... Soon the bespectacled maid and the barren woman were deep in examination of Rebecca Kerr's letter to Ulick Shannon. Into their minds was beginning to leap a terrible joy as they read the lines it had cost Rebecca immense torture to write.

"This is great, this is great!" said the ancient postmistress, clicking her tongue continually in satisfaction. "The cheek of her, mind you, not to send it by the public post like another. But I knew well there was something quare when I saw her calloguing with Thomas James at the market square."

"Wasn't she the sly, hateful, little thing. Why you'd never have thought it of her?"

"A grand person indeed to have in charge of little, innocent girls!"

"Indeed I shouldn't like to have a child if I thought it was to a purty thing like that she'd be sent to school!"

"Nor me," said the old lady, from whom the promise of motherhood had departed for many a long year.

They shook in righteous anger and strong detestation of the sin of Rebecca Kerr, and together they held council as to what might be the best thing to do? They closed the letter, and Mrs. Brannagan again stuck it into her bosom.... What should they do? The children must be saved from contamination anyhow.... An approach to solution of the difficulty immediately presented itself, for there was Mrs. Wyse herself just passing down the street with her ass-load of children. Mrs. Brannagan rushed out of the office and called:

"Mrs. Wyse, I want to see you in private for just a minute!"

The schoolmistress bent over the back of the trap, and they whispered for several minutes. At last, out of her shocked condition, Mrs. Wyse was driven to exclaim:

"Well now, isn't that the limit?"

It seemed an affront to her authority that another should have first discovered it, so she was anxious to immediately recover her lost position of superiority.

"Sure I was having my suspicions of her since ever she come back from the Christmas holidays, and even Monica McKeon too, although she's a single girl and not supposed to know. It's a terrible case, Mrs. Brannagan."

"Terrible, Mrs. Wyse. One of the terriblest ever happened in the valley.... And before the children and all."

"God bless and save us! But we must only leave it in Father O'Keeffe's hands. He'll know what is best to do, never fear. I'll send for him as soon as I get to the school."

There was a note of mournful resignation in her tones as she moved away in the ass-trap with her children, like an old hen in the midst of her brood.... There was a peculiar smirk of satisfaction about the lips of Mrs. Brannagan as she returned to the shop, bent upon sending the letter on its way once more.

"Much good it'll do her now, the dirty little fool!" she said in the happiness of some dumb feeling of vengeance against one who was merely a woman like herself. But she was a woman who had never had a child.

Thomas James was considerably drunk. He had spent the remainder of the shilling upon porter, and Mr. Brannagan had stood him another pint.

"Be sure and deliver it safely now, *for maybe it's important*!" said Mrs. Brannagan, as she returned the letter.

"It's a great letter anyhow. It's after getting me nine pints. That's long over half-a-crown's worth of drink," he said, laughing foolishly as he wandered out to do his errand.

It was a hard journey across the rising meadows to the house of Myles Shannon, where dwelt his nephew Ulick. Thomas James fell many times and wallowed in the tall, green grass, and he fell as he went leaping high hedges, and cut his hands and tore his red face with briars until it was streaked with blood. He was, therefore, an altogether deplorable figure when he at last presented himself at the house of Myles Shannon. Mr. Shannon came to the door to meet him, and in his fuddled condition he laughed to himself as he fished the letter out of his pocket. It was covered red with blood where he had felt it with his torn hand from time to time to see whether or not he still retained possession of it.

"From Mr. Brannagan, I suppose," said Mr. Shannon, thinking it had been written hurriedly by the victualler just fresh from the slaughterhouse and that it was a request for prime beef or mutton from the rich fields of Scarden. He opened it, for his nephew's name on the envelope could not be seen through the blood-stains. He did not notice that it began "My dearest Ulick" until he read down to the sentences that gave him pause.... Thomas James was coughing insinuatingly beside him, so he took half-a-crown from his pocket and handed it to the bedraggled messenger. It was a tremendous reward, and the man of porter did not fully perceive it until he had slipped out into the sunlight.

"Be the Holy Farmer!" he stuttered, "another half-crown's worth of drink, and I after drinking long more than that already. That was the best letter I ever got to carry in me life. A few more like it and I'd either get me death of drink or be a millionaire like John D. Rockefeller or Andrew Carnegie!"

Inside the parlor Myles Shannon was reading Rebecca Kerr's letter with blanched face.... Here was a terrible thing; here had come to him this great trouble for the second time. Something the like of this had happened twenty-five or six years ago, when his brother had been in the same case with Nan Byrne. Curious how it should be repeating itself now! He pondered it for a few moments in its hereditary aspect. But there was more in it than that. There was the trace of his own hand determining it. He had encouraged his nephew with this girl. He had directed him into many reckless ways just that he might bring sorrow to the heart of Nan Byrne in the destruction of her son. It was a wicked thing for him to have done. His own nephew—just to satisfy his desire for revenge. And at the bottom of things he loved his nephew even as he had loved his brother Henry. But he would try to save him the results, the pains and penalties of his infatuation, even as he had tried to save his brother Henry the results of his. But the girl and her fate.... He would not be able to forget that until his dying day.... For it was he who had done this thing entirely, done it in cold blood too because he had heard that John Brennan had soft eyes for Rebecca Kerr and that, to encourage his nephew and produce a certain rivalry, might be the very best means of ruining the fair promise of Nan Byrne's son.

Only last night he had heard from Ulick that John Brennan had entered the college at Ballinamult and that his prospects never looked so good as at present.... To think of that now was to see how just it was that his scheme should have so resulted, for it had been constructed upon a very terrible plan. He had done it to avenge his defeated love for one girl, and lo! it had brought another to her ruin.

"Your uncle is a wealthy man." This sentence from the letter burned before him, and he thought for a moment that here appeared the full solution of the difficulty. But no. Of what use was that when the dread thing was about to happen to her?... But for all that he would send her money to-day or to-morrow, in some quiet way, and tell her the truth and beseech her to go away before the final disgrace of discovery fell upon her. His nephew must not know. He was too young to marry now, least of all, a compulsory marriage after this fashion to a schoolmistress. It was an ascent in the social standing of the girl surely, for his brother Henry had disgraced himself with a mere dressmaker. But any connection beyond the regrettable and painful mistake of the whole thing was out of the question because, for long years, the Shannons had been almost gentlemen in the valley.

Ulick came into the room now.

"Anything strange, uncle?"

"Oh, nothing at all, only a letter from Mr. Brannagan about—about the sheep. I suppose you're not going anywhere to-day. Please don't, for I want you to give me a hand with the lambs after the shearing. And to-night I'll want you to help me with some letters and accounts that I've let slip for ever so long. I want you particularly."

"All right, uncle!"

How tractable and obliging his nephew had become ...! Last summer he would not do a thing like this for any amount of coaxing. He would have business in the valley at all times. But there was a far Power that adjusted matters beyond the plans of men. Ulick had drifted out of the room and Mr. Shannon again took the letter from his pocket. The sight of the blood upon it still further helped the color of his thoughts towards terror.... He crossed hurriedly to the bureau and slipped it beneath the elastic band which held his letters from Helena Cooper, and Mrs. Brennan's letter to her, and Mrs. Brennan's letter to his dead brother Henry.... It seemed to belong there by right of the sad quality which is the distinction of all shattered dreams.... And, just imagine, he had considered his a wonderful scheme of revenge! But now it seemed a poor and a mean thing. He could hardly think of it as a part of the once proud, easy-going Myles Shannon, but rather the bitter and ugly result of some devilish prompting that had come to him here in the lone stretches of his life in this quiet house among the trees.

CHAPTER XXIX

More than ever on this morning was Rebecca aware that the keen eye of Mrs. Wyse was upon her as she moved about the schoolroom. One of the bigger girls was despatched to the other school for Monica McKeon and Master Donnellan's assistant came in to Mrs. Wyse. She nodded the customary greeting to Rebecca as she passed in. This interview was unusual at such an early hour of the day. But it was never the custom of either of them to tell her of what they were talking. As she busied herself teaching the very smallest of the children she felt that the eyes of both women were upon her.

After what appeared to be a very long time Monica passed out. On this second occasion she looked loftily across her glasses and gave no nod of acknowledgment to Rebecca. Rebecca blushed at this open affront. She felt that Mrs. Wyse must have something against her, something she had told Monica just now.... And now the principal was exceedingly busy with her pen as if writing a hurried note.... Rebecca heard the high, coarse voice raised in command:

"Euphemia McGoldrick, I want you!"

Then came the timid "Yes, ma'am!" of Euphemia.

"Here are two letters, child. Take this one to Father O'Keeffe, your parish priest, and this to your mother, like a good child."

"Yes'm!"

Some fear of unknown things began to stir in the breast of Rebecca. This connection of Mrs. McGoldrick with Mrs. Wyse's occupation of the morning seemed to announce some dragging of her into the matter. But as yet, although her mind moved tremulously in its excitement, she had, curiously enough, no suspicion of what was about to happen. It could not be that Mrs. Wyse had suspected. Oh, not at all. There was still no danger. But it might be a near thing.... Already she had begun to wonder would Ulick come to-night. But of course he would come. He was not such a bad fellow. And he might be taken up with his own condition just now. He had missed his examination in Dublin: missed it, maybe, through his foolishness in coming to see her.... But already she had thoroughly blamed herself for this.... To ease the pain of her mind she went busily about her work. She knew that the eye of Mrs. Wyse was upon her and that the very best way of defeating it was by putting on this air of industry. The day, in its half-hour divisions, was passing rapidly towards noon.

A little girl came quickly in to say that Father O'Keeffe was coming up the road. Rebecca glanced out of the window and, sure enough, there he was upon his big, fat, white horse coming into the yard. She heard his loud cries calling into the Boys' School "for a chap to come out and hold his horse." When the boy came to do his bidding he held forth at great length upon the best way of leading "King Billy" around the yard.

Then the reverend manager of Tullahanogue Schools moved into the female portion of the establishment. At the door he twisted his round face into an aspect of severity which was still humorous in its alien incongruity. Here also he removed his hat from his head, which was white and bald like the apex of an egg above the red curve of his countenance. It was his custom to visit the schools of which he was manager, thus precociously to make up in some way for what he lacked in educational knowledge and enthusiasm. As his short, squat figure moved up the passage by the desks, the massive head bowed low upon the broad chest and the fat fingers of both hands coiled behind his back, he was not at all unlike an actor made up as Napoleon Bonaparte. His voice was disciplined in the accents of militarism and dictatorship.

Rebecca noticed on the instant that to-day he was as one intensified. He began to slap his legs continuously with his silver-mounted riding whip. He did not speak to her as he passed in. But, although it caused her heart to flutter for a moment, this appeared to her as no unusual occurrence. He never took notice of her unless when she called at the vestry after Mass upon occasion to deliver up a slice of her salary in Dues and Offerings. Then the Napoleonic powerfulness disappeared and he fell to talking, with laughter in his words, about the richness of Royal Meath in comparison with the wild barrenness of Donegal.

He moved up to where Mrs. Wyse was at work. Rebecca could distinctly hear the loud "Well, what's your best news?" with which he always prefaced his conversations. In low whispers they began to communicate.... It was not till now that she began to have immense doubts as to the purpose of his visit, and already she was trembling in presence of the little children.

"An example of her, Father!"

"Oh yes, an example of her. Nothing less, Mrs. Wyse!"

The words came down to Rebecca clearly through the deep silence that had fallen upon the school since the entrance of Father O'Keeffe. The bigger girls were listening, listening in a great hush of patience for all that had to be reported when they went home. Each one was preparing for her respective examination—

"Was there any one in the school to-day?"

"Yes, mother!"

"Who, the inspector?"

"No, the Priest!"

"Father O'Keeffe?"

"Well, anything else?"

"He was talking to Mrs. Wyse."

"And what was he saying?"

"I couldn't hear, mother, so I couldn't."

"And why didn't you listen? What am I slaving myself to send you to school for?"

And so they were listening with such eagerness now. They were looking down at Rebecca as if she were the object of the whole discussion. Her thoughts were beginning to well into a swirling unconsciousness.... Great sounds, like those of roaring cataracts and the drumming of mighty armies were rolling up to her ears.

Father O'Keeffe and Mrs. Wyse now came down the schoolroom together. As they passed Rebecca, Father O'Keeffe beckoned to her with his riding-whip in the way one might call to a very inferior hireling. Shaken by unique and powerful impulses, she went out into the hall-way to meet her superiors.... Instantaneously she knew what had happened—they knew.

"Well, isn't this a nice thing?" began Father O'Keeffe.

"Ye might say it's a nice thing, Father!" echoed Mrs. Wyse.

"An enormous thing!"

"A terrible thing! Father!"

"You're a nice lady!" he said, addressing Rebecca angrily. "To come into a parish where there is none save decent people to leave a black disgrace upon it and you going away!"

"Was ever the like known, Father? And just imagine her keeping it so secret. Why we thought there was nothing in this affair with Ulick Shannon. There was such an amount of cuteness in the way they used to meet at times and in places we never knew of. In the woods, I suppose!"

Father O'Keeffe was addressing her directly again.

"Why, when I think of the disgrace to this school and all that, it drives me near mad."

"And, mind you, the shocking insult it is to me and to the little children."

"The shocking insult to you and to the little children. True for you, Mrs. Wyse."

"And when I think of how you have contrived to besmirch the fair name of one of the fine, respectable families of the parish, gentlemen, as you might say, without one blot upon their escutcheon."

"People as high up as the Houlihans of Clonabroney."

"People as high up as the Houlihans of Clonabroney, Mrs. Wyse."

His eye was upon Rebecca with a sudden gleam.

"When I think of that, I consider it an enormous offense...." She did not flinch before them. She was thinking only of the way in which they had come to hear it.... She was concerned now that Ulick should not suffer, that his grand family name should not be dragged down with hers.... If he had not come to her she would have slipped away without a word.... And now to think that it had become public. The previous burning of her mind had been nothing to this.... But Father O'Keeffe was still speaking:

"Listen to me, girl! You are to go from hence, but not, as you may imagine, to the place from whence you came. For this very evening I intend to warn your pastor of your lapse from virtue while in our midst, so that you may not return to your father's house and have no more hope of teaching in any National school within the four seas of Ireland."

"That is only right and proper, Father!" put in Mrs. Wyse.

Rebecca was not listening or else she might have shuddered within the shadow of the torture his words held for her. In these moments she had soared far beyond them.... Through the high mood in which she was accepting her tragedy she was becoming exalted.... What glorious moments there would be, what divine compensation in whispering of the torture surrounding its beginning to the little child when it came?

"So now, Rebecca Kerr, I command you to go forth from this school and from the little children that you corrupt towards your own abomination by further presence among them."

As he moved angrily out of the school she moved quietly, and without speaking a word, to take her coat and hat down from the rack.

"Oh, wait!" commanded Mrs. Wyse, "you must not leave until three, until you have made an example of yourself here in a way that all the children may bring home the story. God knows it will be the hard thing for them to be telling their mothers when they go home. The poor little things!"

Rebecca stood there desolately alone in the hall-way through the remainder of the afternoon. In one aspect she appeared as a bold child being thus corrected by a harsh superior. On many more occasions than appeared absolutely necessary Monica McKeon passed and repassed her there as she stood so lonely. The assistant of the Boys' School was a model of disdain as, with her lip curled, she looked away out over her glasses. And ever and anon Mrs. Wyse passed in and out, muttering mournfully to herself:

"The cheek of that now, before the children and all!"

And the elder girls moved about her in a procession of sneering. They knew, and they were examining her for the purpose of giving full accounts when they went home.

But, occasionally, some of the little ones would come and gaze up into her eyes with wild looks. Although they did not know why, they seemed to possess for her an immense, mute pity.

"Poor Miss Kerr!" they would say, stroking her dress, but their big sisters would come and whisk them away.

"Don't touch her. She's dirty——" Then Monica would pass again. At last she heard the merciful stroke of three.

———————————————————

CHAPTER XXX

When John Brennan went to his room after his father's outburst it was with the intention of doing some preparation for the morrow's work at the college; but although he opened several books in turn, he could feel no quickening of knowledge in his mind.... There she was again continually recurring to his thoughts. And now she was far grander. This was the fear that had always been hidden in his heart,—that somehow her friendship with Ulick was not a thing that should have happened. But he had considered it a reality he could not attempt to question. Yet he knew that but for Ulick she must be very near to him. And Ulick had admitted his unworthiness, and so the separation was at an end.

It was surprising that this should have happened now. His mind sprang back to all that tenderness with which his thoughts of her had been surrounded through these long days of dreaming, when he had contrived to meet her, as if by accident, on her way from school.

All through the next day his heart was upon her; the thought of her would give peace. Into every vacant moment she would come with the full light of her presence. He had suddenly relapsed into the mood that had imprisoned him after the summer holidays. He stood aloof from Father Considine and did not wish to see him through the whole of his long day in the college at Ballinamult.... All the way home he pictured her. She was luring him now as she had always lured him—towards a fairer vision of the valley.

He noticed how the summer was again flooding over the fields like a great river spilling wide. It was a glorious coincidence that she should be returning to him now, a creature of brightness at a time of beauty.

The road seemed short this pleasant afternoon, and the customary feeling of dusty weariness was not upon him as he leapt lightly off the bicycle at his mother's door. Mrs. Brennan came out to meet him eagerly. This was no unusual occurrence now that he had again begun to ascend the ladder of the high condition she had planned for him. She was even a far prouder woman now, for, somehow, she had always half remembered the stain of charity hanging over his uprise in England. Besides this he was nearer to her, moving intimately through the valley, a living part of her justification.... Her fading eyes now looked out tenderly at her son. There seemed to be a great light in them this afternoon, a great light of love for him.... He was moved beneath their gaze. And still she continued to smile upon him in a weak way as within the grip of some strong excitement. He saw when he entered that his dinner was not set out as usual on the white table in the kitchen.... She brought him into the sewing-room. And still she had the same smile trembling upon her lips and the same light in her eyes.... All this was growing mysterious and oppressive. But his mood was proof against sad influences. It must be some tale of good fortune come to their house of which his mother had now to tell.

"D'ye know what, John? The greatest thing ever is after happening!"

"Is that a fact, mother?"

"Though mebbe 'tis not right for me to tell you and you all as one as a priest, I may say. But sure you're bound to hear it, and mebbe a little knowledge of the kind might not be amiss even to one in your exalted station. And then to make it better, it concerns two very near friends of yours, Mr. Ulick Shannon and Miss Rebecca Kerr, I thank you!"

John Brennan's mind leaped immediately to interest. Were they gone back to one another, and after what he had thought to-day? This was the question his lips carried inwardly to himself.

"I don't know how I can tell you. But Father O'Keeffe was at school to-day in a great whet. He made a show of her before the children, Mrs. Wyse and Miss McKeon, of course, giving him good help. He dismissed her, and told her to go about her business. He'll mebbe speak of her publicly from the altar on Sunday."

"And what is it, mother, what—?"

"Oh, she's going to have a misfortune, me son. She's going to be a mother, God bless us all! and not married or a ha'porth!"

"O God!"

"But sure she put in for nothing else, with her going up and all that to Dublin to have her dresses made, instead of getting them done nice and quiet and modest and respectable be me. I may tell you that I was more than delighted to hear it."

"Well now, and the—"

John was biting his lips in passion, but she took another view of it as she interrupted him.

"Ah, you may well ask who *he* is, who but that scoundrel Ulick Shannon, that I was never done asking you not to speak to. You were young and innocent, of course, and could not be expected to know what I know. But mebbe you'll avoid him now, although I think he won't be long here, for mebbe Father O'Keeffe'll run him out of the parish. Maybe not though, for his uncle has bags of money. Indeed I wouldn't put it apast him if *he* was the lad encouraged him to this, for the Shannons were always blackguards in their hearts.... But it'll be great to hear Father O'Keeffe on Sunday. I must be sure and go to his Mass. Oh, it'll be great to hear him!"

"Yes, I suppose it will be great to hear him."

John spoke out of the gathering bitterness of his heart.

"I wonder what'll become of her now. I wonder where'll she go. Oh, to Dublin, I suppose. She was always fond of it."

His mother was in a very ecstasy of conjecture as to the probable extent of Rebecca's fate. And this was the woman who had always expressed a melting tenderness in her actions towards him. This was his mother who had spoken now with all uncharitableness. There was such an absence of human pity in her words as most truly appalled him.... Very quickly he saw too that it was upon his own slight connection with this tragic thing her mind was dwelling. This was to him now a token, not of love, but rather of enormous selfishness.... Her eyes were upon him still, watering in admiration with a weak gleam.... The four walls seemed to be moving in to crush him after the manner of some medieval torture chamber.... Within them, too, was beginning to rise a horrid stench as of dead human things.... This ghastliness that had sprung up between mother and son seemed to have momentarily blotted out the consciousness of both. They stared at one another now with glassy, unseeing eyes.

After three Rebecca took her lonely way from the school. Neither Mrs. Wyse nor Monica McKeon had a word for her at parting. Neither this woman, who was many times a mother, nor this girl who might yet be a mother many times. They were grinning loudly and passing some sneer between them, as they moved away from one another alone.

Down the valley road she went, the sunlight dazzling her tired eyes. A thought of something that had happened upon this day last year came with her remembrance of the date. It was the first anniversary of some slight, glad event that had brought her happiness, and yet what a day it was of dire happening? Just one short year ago she had not known the valley or Ulick or this fearful thing.... There were friends about her on this day last year and the sound of laughter, and she had not been so far distant from her father's house. And, O God! to think that now she was so much alone.

Suddenly she became aware that there was some one running by her side and calling "Miss Kerr! Miss Kerr!"

"Oh, Janet Comaskey!" she said, turning. "Is it you?"

"Yes, Miss Kerr. I want to tell you that I was talking to God last night, and I was telling Him about you. He asked me did I like you, and I said I did. 'And so do I,' said He. 'I like Miss Kerr very much,' He said, 'for she's very nice, very, very nice.'"

Rebecca had never disliked this queer child, but she loved her now, and bending down, warmly kissed her wild face.

"Thanks, miss. I only wanted to tell you about God," said Janet, dropping behind.

Rebecca was again alone, but now she was within sight of the house of Sergeant McGoldrick. It seemed to be dozing there in the sunlight. She began to question herself did those within already know ...? Now that the full publicity of her condition seemed imminent an extraordinary feeling of vanity was beginning to take possession of her. She took off her dust-coat and hung it upon her arm. Thus uncloaked she would face the eyes of Mrs. McGoldrick and her daughters, Euphemia and Clementina, and the eyes, very probably, of John Ross McGoldrick and Neville Chamberlain McGoldrick....

But when she entered the house she experienced the painful stillness of a tomb-like place. There was no one to be seen. She went upstairs with a kind of faltering in her limbs, but her head was erect and her fine eyes were flashing.... Even still was she soaring beyond and beyond them. Her eye was caught by a note pinned upon her door. It seemed very funny and, despite her present condition of confusion and worry, she smiled, for this was surely a melodramatic trick that Mrs. McGoldrick had acquired from the character of her reading.... Still smiling, she tore it open. It read like a proclamation, and was couched in the very best handwriting of Sergeant McGoldrick.

> "Miss Kerr,
>
> Rev. Louis O'Keeffe, P.P., Garradrimna, has given notice that, on account of certain deplorable circumstances, we are to refuse you permission to lodge with us any longer. This we hasten to do without any regret, considering that, to oblige you at the instigation of Father O'Keeffe, we broke the Regulation of the Force, which forbids the keeping of lodgers by any member of that body. We hereby give you notice to be out of this house by 6 p.m. on this evening, May —, 19—, having, it is understood, by that time packed up your belongings and discharged your liabilities to Mrs. McGoldrick. Father O'Keeffe has, very magnanimously, arranged that Mr. Charles Clarke is to call for you with his

motor and take you with all possible speed to the station at
Kilaconnaghan.

Sylvester McGoldrick (Sergeant, R.I.C.)."

The official look of the pronouncement seemed only to increase its gloomy
finality, but the word "magnanimously," fresh from the dictionary at the
Barrack, made her laugh outright. The offense she had committed was
unnamed, too terrible for words. She was being sentenced like a doomed
Easter rebel.... Yet, even still, she was not without some thought of the
practical aspect of her case. She owed thirty shillings to Mrs. McGoldrick.
This would leave her very little, out of the few pounds she had saved from
her last instalment of salary, with which to face the world. This, of course, if
Ulick did not come.... And here was her dinner, set untidily in the stuffy room
where the window had not been opened since the time she had left it this
morning in confusion. And the whole house was quiet as the grave. She never
remembered to have heard it so quiet at any other time. It seemed as if all
this silence had been designed with a studied calculation of the pain it would
cause. There was no kindness in this woman either, although she too was a
mother and had young daughters. It appeared so greatly uncharitable that in
these last terrible moments she could not cast from her the small and pitiful
enmity she had begun upon the evening of Rebecca's arrival in the valley. She
would not come even now and help her pack up her things, and she so
weary?... But it was easily done. The few articles that had augmented her
wardrobe since her coming to the valley would go into the basket she had
used to carry those which were barely necessary for her comfort when she
went to that lonely cottage in Donegal.... The mean room was still bare as
when she had first come to it. She had not attempted to decorate it. In a pile
in one corner stood the full series of *Irish School Weeklies* and *Weldon's Ladies'
Journals* she had purchased since her coming here. She had little use for either
of these publications now, little use for the one that related to education or
the other that related to adornment.

There came a feverish haste upon her to get done with her preparations for
departure, and soon they were completed. She had her trunk corded and all
ready. She had no doubt that Ulick would meet her upon The Road of the
Dead at 5.30, the hour she had named in the letter of this morning. It was
lucky she had so accurately guessed her possible time of departure, although
somehow she had had no notion this morning of leaving so soon. But already
it was more than 4.30 by her little wristlet watch. She put on her best dress,
which had been left out on the bed, and redid her hair. It was still the certain
salvage from the wreck she was becoming. Ulick or any other man, for all he
had ruined her, must still love her for that hair of gold. It needed no crown
at all, but a woman's vanity was still hers, and she put on a pretty hat which
Ulick had fancied in Dublin. She had worn it for the first time last summer

in Donegal, and it became her better than any hat she had ever worn.... What would they say if they saw her moving about in this guise, so brazenly as it seemed, when she might be spoken of from the altar on Sunday?

Now fell upon her a melancholy desire to see the chapel. There was yet time to go there and pray just as she had thought of praying on her first evening on coming to Garradrimna. She took a final glance at the little, mean room. It had not been a room of mirth for her, and she was not sorry to leave it— there was the corded trunk to tell the tale of its inhospitality. She took the money for Mrs. McGoldrick from her purse and put it into an envelope.... Going downstairs she left it upon the kitchen table. There was no one to be seen, but she could hear the scurrying of small feet from her as if she were some monstrous and forbidden thing.

As she went up the bright road there was a flickering consciousness in her breast that she was an offense against the sunlight, but this feeling fled away from her when she went into the chapel and knelt down to pray. Her mind was full of her purpose, and she did not experience the distraction of one single, selfish thought. But when she put her hands up to her face in an attitude of piety she felt that her face was burning.

It was a day for confessions, but there were few people in the chapel, and those not approaching the confessionals. The two young curates, Father Forde and Father Fagan, were moving about the quiet aisles, each deeply intent upon the reading of his office. They were nearer the altar than to her, but for all the air of piety in which they seemed to be enveloped, they detected her presence immediately and simultaneously. Soon they began to extend their back and forward pacing to include her within the range of their sidelong vision.... By the time she had got half way around her little mother-of-pearl rosary they were moving past her and towards one another at her back. She was saying her poor prayers as well as she could, but there they were with their heads working up and down as they looked alternately at her and at their holy books.... Just as she got to the end of the last decade she was conscious that they had come together and were whispering behind her.... It was not until then that she saw the chapel for what it stood in regard to her. It was the place where, on Sunday next, mean people would smirk in satisfaction as they sat listening in all their lack of charity and fulness of pride.... The realization brought the pulsing surge of anger to her blood and she rose to come away. But when she turned around abruptly there were the two curates with their eyes still fixed upon her.... She did not meet their looks full straight, for they turned away as if to avoid the contamination of her as she ran from the House of God.

When John Brennan reached a point in his disgust where further endurance was impossible he broke away from the house and from his mother. He went out wildly through the green fields.

But he would see her. He would go to her, for surely she had need of him now.... If Ulick did not come.... And there was much in his manner and conversation of the previous night to make it doubtful.... If he did not take her away from this place and make her his own to protect and cherish, there was only one course left open.... He knew little of these things, for he knew little of the ways of life, but instinctively he felt that Rebecca would now cling to Ulick and that Ulick would be a great scoundrel if he spurned her from him. And what, he asked himself, would he, John Brennan, do in that case?

No answer would spring directly to his thoughts, but some ancient, primeval feeling was stirring in his heart—the answer that men have held to be the only answer from the beginning of the world. But that was a dreadful thing which, in its eddying circles of horror, might compass his own end also.

But, maybe the whole story was untrue. He had heard his mother speak many a time after the same fashion, and there was never one case of the kind but had proved untrue. Yet it was terrible that no answer would come flashing out from his wild thoughts, and already he had reached The Road of the Dead.

His wandering eyes had at last begun to rest upon a wide, green field. He saw the wind and sun conspiring to ripple the grass into the loveliest little waves. He had loved this always, and even the present state of his mind did not refuse the sensation of its beauty. He went and leaned across the field gate to gaze upon it.

He turned suddenly, for there was a step approaching him along the road. Yes, surely it was she. It was Rebecca Kerr herself coming towards him down The Road of the Dead.... She was smiling, but from the dark, red shadows about her eyes it was easy to see that she had quite recently been crying.

"Good evening, John Brennan!" she said.

"Good evening, Miss Kerr!"

There was a deep touch of concern, turning to anxiety, almost a rich tenderness in his words. She heard them for what they were, and there came to her clearly their accents of pity.... For the moment neither seemed capable of finding speech.... Her eyes were searching The Road of the Dead for the man she expected to meet her here. But he was not coming. In the silence that had fallen between them John Brennan had clearly glimpsed the dumb longing that was upon her.... He felt the final gloom that was moving in around her ... yet he could not find speech.

"I'm going away from the valley," said Rebecca.

He made some noise in his throat, but she could hear no distinct word.

"It was not *you* I expected to meet here this evening. It is so strange how we have met like this."

"I just came out for a walk," he stammered, at a loss for something better to say.

"I'm glad we have met," she said, "for this is the last time."

It was easy to see that her words held much meaning for herself and him.... He seemed to be nearer the brink as her eyes turned from him again to search the road.

"He will not come," she said, and there was a kind of wretched recklessness in her tones. "I know he will not come, for that possibility has never been." She grew more resigned of a sudden. She saw that John Brennan too was searching the road with his eyes.... Then he knew the reason why she was going away.

He was such a nice boy, and between his anxious watching now for her sake he was gazing with pity into her eyes.... He must know Ulick too as a man knows his friend, and that Ulick would not come to her in this her hour of trial.... The knowledge seemed the more terrible since it was through John Brennan it had come; and yet it was less terrible since he did not disdain her for what she had done. She saw through his excuse. He had come this way with the special purpose of seeing her, and if he had not met her thus accidentally he must inevitably have called at the house of Sergeant McGoldrick to extend his farewell. She was glad that she had saved him this indignity by coming out to her own disappointment.... She was sorry that he had again returned to his accustomed way of thinking of her, that he had again departed from the way into which she had attempted to direct him.

And now there loomed up for her great terror in this thought. Yet she could read it very clearly in the way he was looking so friendly upon her.... Why had he always looked upon her in this way? Surely she had never desired it. She had never desired him. It was Ulick she had longed for always. It was Ulick she had longed for this evening, and it was John Brennan who had come.... Yes, how well he had come? It was very simple and very beautiful, this action of his, but in its simple goodness there was a fair promise of its high desolation. It appeared that she stood for his ruin also, and, even now, in the mounting moments of her fear, this appeared as an ending far more appalling.... She was coming to look at her own fate as a thing she might be able to bear, but there was something so vastly filled with torture in this thought.... Whenever she would look into the eyes of the child and make plans for its little future she would think of John Brennan and what had happened to him.

She felt that they had been a long time standing here at this gate, by turns gazing anxiously up and down the road, by turns looking vacantly out over the sea of grass. Time was of more account than ever before, for was it not upon this very evening that she was being banished from the valley?

"I must go now," she said; "*he* will never come."

He did not answer, but moved as if to accompany her.... She grew annoyed as she observed his action.

"No, no, you must not come with me now. You must not speak with me again. I have placed myself forever beyond your friendship or your thought!"

As she extended her hand to him her heart was moved by a thousand impulses.

"Good-by, John Brennan!" she said simply.

"Good-by, Rebecca!" said he at last, finding speech by a tremendous effort.... And without another word they parted there on The Road of the Dead.

Outside the garden gate of Sergeant McGoldrick Charlie Clarke was waiting for her with his motor-car. Her trunk had been put in at the back. This was an unholy job for a saintly chauffeur, but it was Father O'Keeffe's command and his will must be done. When the news of it had been communicated to him he had said a memorable thing:

"Well, now, the quare jobs a religious man has sometimes to do; but maybe these little punishments are by way of satisfaction for some forgotten and far-distant sin!"

Rebecca understood his anxiety to have her off his hands as she saw him jump in behind the wheel at her approach. She got in beside her poor trunk, and presently the car would be ready to start. There was not a trace of any of the McGoldrick family to be seen.... But there was a sudden breaking through the green hedge upon the other side of the road, and Janet Comaskey stood beside the car. Rebecca was surprised by the sudden appearance of the little, mad girl at this moment.

"Miss Kerr, Miss Kerr!" she called. "I got this from God. God told me to give you this!"

The car started away, and Rebecca saw that the superscription on the letter she had been handed was in the pronounced Vere Foster style of Master Donnellan. Doubtless it was some long-winded message of farewell from the kind-hearted master, and she would not open it now. It would be something to read as she moved away towards Dublin.

Just now her eyes were being filled by the receding pageant of the valley, that place of all earth's places which had so powerfully arrayed its villainy against her.... And to think that he had not come.... It was the Valley of Hinnom.... Yes, to think that he had not come after all she had been to him, after all the love of her heart she had given him. No word could ever, ever pass between them again. They were upon the very brink of the eternity of separation. She knew now that for all the glory in which she had once beheld him, he must shrivel down to the bitter compass of a little, painful memory. Oh, God! to think he had not replied to her letter, and the writing of it had given her such pain.

They were at the station of Kilaconnaghan. Charlie Clarke had not spoken all through the journey, but now he came up to her indignantly, as if very vexed for being compelled to speak to her at all, and said: "The fare is one pound!"

The words smote her with a little sense of shock. She had been expecting something by way of climax. She was very certain in her consciousness that the valley would not let her slip thus quietly away.—A pound for the journey, although it was Father O'Keeffe who had engaged the car.—She must pay this religious robber a huge price for the drive. There rushed through her mind momentarily a mad flash of rebellion. The valley was carrying its tyranny a little too far.... She would not pay.... But almost immediately she was searching for a note in her purse.... There were so very few of them now. Yet she could not leave the valley with any further little stain upon her. They would talk of a thing like this for years and years.

With a deadly silence hanging over him and fearful thoughts coming into his mind Myles Shannon had kept himself and his nephew Ulick at work all through the day. After tea in the lonely dining-room he fetched in his inky account books, which had been neglected for many a month. His nephew would here have work to occupy him for the remainder of the evening and probably far into the night. Ulick was glad of the task, for his mind was very far from being at ease.

Then Mr. Shannon took £100 from the old-fashioned bureau in the parlor, which held, with the other things, all his papers and accounts, and while the evening was yet high went down towards the house of Sergeant McGoldrick to see Rebecca Kerr. Around a bend of the road he encountered Charlie Clarke on his way back from Kilaconnaghan, where he had been delayed upon bazaar business.

The saintly chauffeur at once put on the brakes. This was Mr. Myles Shannon and some one worth speaking to. He bowed a groveling salute.

"You're out pretty late?" said Mr. Shannon.

"Oh, yes!" And then he went on to describe his work of the evening. He felt inclined to offer his condolence to Mr. Shannon in a most respectful whisper, but thought better of it at the last moment.

"And no one knows where she has gone?"

"No one. She has disappeared from the valley."

"She went away very suddenly."

"Yes, Father O'Keeffe saw that, in the public interest, she should disappear after this fashion. The motor was a help, you know."

Charlie Clarke offered to drive Mr. Shannon to his home. No word passed between them as they drew up the avenue to the lonely house among the trees.

In the train, moving on towards Dublin, Rebecca Kerr had just opened the letter from Master Donnellan. It contained a £5 note.... This was like a cry of mercy and pardon for the valley.... The rich fields of Meath were racing by.

CHAPTER XXXI

There was a curious hush about the lake next evening, although the little cottage of Hughie Murtagh was swept by winds which stirred mournfully through all the bright abundance of early summer. Even the orange-blossoms of the furze seemed to put on an aspect of surrender. There was no challenge in their color now; they looked almost white against a somber sunset. John Brennan moped about among the fir-trees. He came to a stand-still by one that had begun to decay and which was even more mournful in its failure to contribute another plumed head to the general effect of mourning. But it seemed to shake enraged at this impotence in its poor foundation over the deserted warren, from which Shamesy Golliher had long since driven the little rabbits towards that dark Chicago of slaughter which was represented to them by Garradrimna.

The same color of desolation was upon the reeds which separated him from the water. The water itself had, beneath its pretense of brightness upon the surface, the appearance of ooze, as if it had come washing over the slime of dead things.

It was here that John Brennan had come to wait for Ulick Shannon, and, as he waited, his mood became that of his surroundings.... He fell to running over what had happened to him. Alternately, in the swirl of his consciousness, it appeared as the power of the valley and as the Hand of God. Yet, whatever it might be in truth, this much was certain. It had reduced his life to ruins. It was a fearful thing, and he shuddered a little while he endeavored to produce a clear picture of it for the chastisement as well as the morbid excitement of his imagination.

But there came instead a far different picture, which seemed to have the effect of lifting for a moment the surrounding gloom. He saw Rebecca Kerr again as upon many an afternoon they had met. For one brave moment he strove to recover the fine feeling that had filled him at those times. But it would not come. Something had happened, something terrible which soiled and spoiled her forever.

For love of her he had dreamed even unto the desire of defeating his mother's love. And yet there was no triumph in his heart now, nothing save defeat and a great weariness. Neither his mother nor Rebecca Kerr were any longer definite hopes upon which his mind might dwell.... His thoughts were running altogether upon Ulick Shannon. It was for Ulick he waited now in this lonely, wind-swept place, like any villain he had ever seen depicted upon the cover of a penny dreadful in Phillips's window when he was a boy. He now saw himself fixed in his own imagination after this fashion. Ulick Shannon would soon come. There was no doubt of this, for a definite appointment had been made during the day. He had remained at home from the college in Ballinamult to bring it about. Soon they would be endeavoring to enter what must be the final and tragic bye-way of their story. And it must be all so dreadfully interesting, this ending he had planned.... Now the water came flowing towards him more rapidly as if to hurry the tragedy. It came more thickly and muddily and with long, billowy strides as if it yearned to gather some other body still holding life to its wild breast. Its waters kept flowing as if from some wide wound that ached and would not be satisfied; that bled and called aloud for blood forever.

Now also the evening shadows were beginning to creep down the hills and with them a deeper hush was coming upon the wild longing of all things. Yet it was no hush of peace, but rather the concentration of some horrible purpose upon one place.

"I am going away on Friday," Ulick had written in one of the two notes that had been exchanged between them by the messenger during the day, "and I would like to see you for what must, unfortunately, be the last time. I am slipping away unknown to my uncle or to any one, and it is hardly probable that I will be seen in these parts again."

At length he beheld the approach of Ulick down the long Hill of Annus.... His spirit thrilled within him and flamed again into a white flame of love for the girl who was gone.... And coming hither was the man who had done this thing.... The thickest shadows of the evening would soon be gathered closely about the scene they were to witness.... The very reeds were rustling now in dread.

The lake was deep here at the edge of the water.... And in the rabbit-warren beneath his feet were the heavy pieces of lead piping he had transported in the night. He had taken them from his father's stock of plumber's materials, that moldy, unused stock which had so long lain in the back yard and which, in a distant way, possessed an intimate connection with this heaped-up story.... In a little instant of peculiar consciousness he wondered whether it would be pliable enough.... There were pieces for the legs and pieces for the arms which would enfold those members as in a weighty coffin.... And hidden nearer to his hand was the strangely-shaped, uncouth weapon his father had used many a time with such lack of improvement upon the school slates and with which one might kill a man.... The body would rest well down there beneath the muddy waters.... There would be no possibility of suspicion falling upon him, for the story of Rebecca Kerr's disgrace and Ulick Shannon's connection with it had already got about the valley.... He had been listening to his mother telling it to people all day.... Ulick's disappearance, in a way self-effacing and unnamed, was hourly expected. This opportunity appeared the one kind trick of Fate which had been so unkind to the passionate yearnings of John Brennan.

But Ulick Shannon was by his side, and they were talking again as friends of different things in the light way of old.... Their talk moved not at all within the shadows of things about to happen presently.... But the shadows were closing in, and very soon they must fall and lie heavily upon all things here by the lake.

"Isn't it rather wonderful, Brennan, that I should be going hence through the power of a woman? It is very strange how they always manage to have their revenge, how they beat us in the long run no matter how we may plume ourselves on a triumph that we merely fancy. Although we may degrade and rob them of their treasure, ours is the final punishment. Do you remember how I told you on that day we were at the 'North Leinster Arms,' in Ballinamult, there was no trusting any woman? Not even your own mother! Now this Rebecca Kerr, she—"

The sentence was never finished. John Brennan had not spoken, but his hand had moved twice—to lift the uncouth weapon from the foot of the tree and again to strike the blow.... The mold of unhappy clay from which the words of Ulick had just come was stilled forever. The great cry which struggled to break from the lips resulted only in a long-drawn sigh that was like a queer swoon. The mournful screech of a wild bird flying low over the lake drowned the little gust of sound.... Then the last lone silence fell between the two young men who had once been most dear companions.

No qualms of any kind came to the breast of John Brennan. He had hardened his heart between the leaping flames of Love and Hate, and there was upon him now the feeling of one who has done a fine thing. He was in the moment of his triumph, yet he was beginning to be amazed by his sudden power and the result of his decision.... That he, John Brennan, should have had it in him to murder his friend.... But no, it was his enemy he had murdered, the man who had desecrated the beauty of the world.... And there was a rare grandeur in what he had done. It was a thing of beauty snatched from the red hands of Death.

Yet as he went about his preparations for submerging the body he felt something akin to disgust for this the mean business of the murder.... Here was where the beauty that had been his deed snapped finally from existence in his consciousness and disappeared from him.

Henceforth gray thought after gray thought came tumbling into his mind. Ulick had not been a bad fellow. He had tried to be kind to him—all the motor-drives and the walks and talks they had had. Even the bits of days and nights spent together in Garradrimna.... And how was Ulick to know of his affection for Rebecca Kerr? There had never been the faintest statement of the fact between them; his whole manner and conversation and the end for which he was intended forbade any suspicion of the kind. In fact to have had such a doubt would have been a sin in the eyes of many a Catholic.... The legs and arms were well weighted now.... This might not have happened if his mother had been attended in the right spirit of filial obedience.... But with the arrogance of youth, which he now realized for the first time, he had placed himself above her opinion and done what he had desired at the moment. And why had he done so?... She would seem to have had foreboding of all this in the way she had looked upon him so tenderly with her tired eyes many a time since his memorable home-coming last summer. She had always been so fearfully anxious.... Here must have been the melancholy end she had seen at the back of all dreaming.... He could feel that sad look clearly, all dimmed by dark presentiments.

The body was a great weight. He strove to lift it in his arms in such a way that his clothes might not be soiled by the blood.... His face was very near the pale, dead face with the red blood now clotting amongst the hair.... He was almost overpowered by his burden as he dragged it to the water's edge.... It was a very fearful thing to look at just as the water closed over it with a low, gurgling sound, as if of mourning, like the cry of the bird in the moment the murder had been done.

As he staggered back from the sighing reeds he noticed that the ground was blood-drenched beneath the tree.... But he was doing the thing most thoroughly. In a frenzy of precautionary industry he began to hack away the earth with the slating implement very much as Shamesy Golliher might hack it in search of a rabbit.

Later he seemed to put on the very appearance of Shamesy himself as, with bent body, he slouched away across the ridge of the world. He too had just effected a piece of slaughter and Garradrimna seemed to call him.

CHAPTER XXXII

When he came out upon the valley road he was no longer the admirable young man he had been less than a year since. He was a broken thing, and he was stained by another's blood. He was marked eternally by what he had done, and there was upon him a degradation unspeakable. He was an offense against existence and against the gathering, blessed gloom of the quiet evening.... He had murdered one who had been his friend, and it was a thing he might never be able to forget. The body, with all the lovely life so recently gone from it, he had weighted and sunk beneath the surface of the lake.... It was down there now, a poor, dead thing among the ooze of dead things from which the water had taken its color and quality. The wild spirit that had been Ulick Shannon, so contradictory in its many aspects, was now soaring lightly aloft upon the wings of clean winds and he, John Brennan, who had effected this grand release, felt the weights still heavy about his heart.

He came on a group of children playing by the roadside. It seemed as if they had been driven across his path to thwart him with their innocence. He instantly remembered that other evening when he had been pained to hear them express the ugly, uncharitable notions of their parents regarding a child of another religion. Now they were playing merrily as God had intended them to play, and religion, with its tyranny of compulsion towards thoughts of death and sin, seemed distant from them, and distant was it from him too. His mind was empty of any thought. Would no kindly piece of imagination come down to cool his spirit with its grace or lift from his heart the oppression of the leaden weights he had bound about the body of Ulick Shannon?... At last he had remembrance of his mother. It had been borne in upon him during some of his lonely cycle-rides to and from Ballinamult that things should not be, somehow, as they were. He was moving along exalted ways while his mother labored in lonely silence at her machine.... Where was the money coming from? Such an unproductive state as his required money for its upkeep. His father was no toiler, but she was always working there alone in the lonely room. Her hands were grown gnarled and hard through her years of labor.... Just presently she was probably discussing a dismal matter of ways and means with some woman of the valley, saying as she had said through the long years:

"Thank God and His Blessed Mother this night, I still have me hands. Aye, that's what I was just saying to Mrs. So and So this morning—Thank God I still have me hands!"

Thus she was going on now, he imagined, as he had always heard her, a pathetic figure sitting there and looking painfully through the heavy, permanent mist that was falling down upon her eyes. And yet it was not thus she really was at this moment. For although it was a woman who held her company, there was no mood of peace between them. It was Marse Prendergast who was with her, and she was proceeding busily with her eternal whine. Mrs. Brennan was now disturbed in her mind and fearful of the great calamity that might happen. While she had bravely maintained the money in the little chest upstairs there had lingered, in spite of every affliction, a sense of quietness and independence. But now she was without help and as one distraught. Of late this gibbering old woman had obtained a certain power over her, and a considerable portion of the once proud Mrs. Brennan had fallen finally away. Although, at unaccountable moments, her strong pride would spring up to dazzle the people of the valley, she did not now possess that remarkable imperviousness which had so distinguished her attitude towards life. Now she was in a condition of disintegration, unable to maintain an antagonism or hide a purpose. The old ruined woman, the broken shuiler of the roads, was beginning to behold the ruins of another woman, the ruins of Mrs. Brennan, who had once been so "thick" and proud.

"So you won't hearken to me request?"

"I can't, Marse dear. I have no money to give you!"

This was a true word, for the little store upstairs had gone this way and that. Tommy Williams had had to be given his interest, and although people might think that John was getting his education for charity, no one knew better than she the heavy fees of the college in Ballinamult. Besides, he must keep up a good appearance in the valley.

But when Marse Prendergast made a demand she knew no reason and could make no allowance.

"Well, Nan, me dear, I must do me duty. I must speak out when you can't bribe me to be silent. I must do a horrid piece of business this night. I must turn a son against his mother. Yes, that must be the way of it now, a son turned for good against his mother. For surely there could be no pardon in his grand, holy eyes for what you were once upon a time. But let me tell you this, that I'd have acquainted him anyhow, for I'd not have gone to me grave with that sin on me no matter what. They say it isn't right to offer a son to God where there's after being any big blemish in the family, and that if you do a woful misfortune or a black curse comes of it. And sure that was the quare, big blemish in your family, Nan Byrne, the quarest blemish ever was."

Mrs. Brennan began to cry. She seemed to have come at last to the end of all her long attempt to brazen things out.... Marse Prendergast was not slow to observe this acceptance of defeat, and saw that now surely was her time to be hard and bitter. She was growing so old, a withered stump upon the brink of years, and there was upon her an enormous craving for a little money.

People were even driven, by her constant whine for this thing and that, to say how she had a little store of her own laid by which she gloated over with a wicked and senile delight. And for what, in God's name, was she hoarding and she an old, lone woman with the life just cross-wise in her?... And it was always Mrs. Brennan whom she had visited with her singular and special persecution.

"I suppose now you think you're the quare, clever one to be going on with your refusals from day to day. I suppose you think I don't know that you have a *chesht* full of money that you robbed from poor Henry Shannon, God be good to him, when he used to be coming running to see you, the foolish fellow!"

"As God's me judge, Marse Prendergast, I haven't e'er a penny in the house. I'm in debt in Garradrimna this blessed minute, and that's as sure as you're there!"

"Go on out of that with your talk of debts, and you to be sending your son John through his college courses before all our eyes like any fine lady in the land. And think of all the grand money you'll be getting bye and bye in rolls and cartloads!"

"Aye, with the help of God!"

Even in the moment of her torment Mrs. Brennan could not restrain her vanity of her son.

"And to think of all that being before you now and still you keep up your mean refusals of the little thing I ask," said the old woman with the pertinacious unreasonableness of age.

"I haven't got the money, Marse, God knows I haven't."

"God knows nothing, Nan Byrne, only your shocking villainy. And 'tis the great sin for you surely. And if God knows this, it is for some one else to know your sin. It is for your son John to know the kind of a mother that he loves and honors."

Mrs. Brennan had heard this threat on many an occasion yet even now the repetition of it made her grow suddenly pale.... An expression of sickliness was upon her face seen even through the shadowed sewing-room. Always this thought had haunted her that some time John might come to know.

"Long threatening comes at last!" was a phrase that had always held for her the darkest meaning. She could never listen to any woman make use of it without shuddering violently. Marse Prendergast had threatened so often and often.

"Ah, no, Nan Byrne, this is something I could never let pass. And all the long days I saw you contriving here at the machine, and you so anxious and attentive, sure I used to be grinning to myself at the thoughts of the bloody fine laugh I'd be having at you some day. I used, that's God's truth!"

It seemed terrible to be told the story of this hate that had been so well hidden, now springing up before her in a withering blast of ingratitude and being borne to her understanding upon such quiet words.... She sighed ever so slightly, and her lips moved gently in the aspiration of a prayer.

"O Jesus, Mary and Joseph!" was what she said.

The pious ejaculation seemed to leap at once towards the accomplishment of a definite purpose, for immediately it had the effect of moving Marse Prendergast towards the door.

"I'm going now!"

The words were spoken with an even more chilling quietness. Mrs. Brennan made a noise as if to articulate something, but no words would come from her.

"And let you not be thinking that 'tis only this little thing I'm going to tell him, for there's a whole lot more. I'm going to tell him *all* I know, *all that I didn't tell you* through the length of the years, though, God knows, it has been often burning me to tell.... You think, I suppose, as clever as you are, that the child was buried in the garden. Well, that's not a fact, nor the color of a fact, for all I've made you afraid of it so often.... Grace Gogarty had no child of her own for Henry Shannon. *Ulick Shannon is your own child that was sold be your ould mother for a few pound!*"

"That's a lie for you, Marse Prendergast!"

"'Tis no lie at all I'm telling you, but the naked truth. I suppose neither of them lads, Ulick nor John, ever guessed the reason why they were so fond of one another, but that was the reason; and 'tis I used to enjoy seeing them together and I knowing it well. Isn't it curious now to say that you're the mother of a blackguard and the mother of the makings of a priest?... Mebbe you'd give me the little bit of money now? Mebbe?"

Mrs. Brennan did not answer. Big tears were rolling down her cheeks one after the other.... Her heart had been rent by this sudden flash of information. Even the last remaining stronghold of her vanity had been swept away. That she, who had claim in her own estimation to be considered the wise woman of the valley, could not have long since guessed at the existence of a fact so intimate.... Her heart was wounded, not unto death, but immortally.... Her son! Ulick Shannon her son! O Mother of God!

John Brennan was still in his agony as he saw the long-tongued shuiler coming towards him down the road. She was making little journeys into the ditches as she came along. She was gathering material for a fire although every bush was green.... She was always shivering at the fall of night. The appearance of the children had filled him with speculations as to where he might look for some comfort.... Could it be derived from the precepts of religion translated into acts of human kindness? Momentarily he was confused as he attempted to realize some act of goodness to be done here and now. He was unable to see.

Old Marse Prendergast, coming towards him slowly, was the solitary link connecting his mind with any thought. To him she appeared the poor old woman in need of pity who was gathering green sticks from the hedge-rows to make her a fire which would not kindle. He remembered that morning, now some time distant, when he had helped her carry home a bundle of her sticks on his way from Mass. It had appeared to him then, as it did now, a Christ-like action, but his mother had rebuked him for it. Yet he had always wished his mother to take the place of Mary when he tried to snatch some comfort from the Gospel story. Soon he was by her side speaking as kindly as he could.... Great fear was already upon him.

"God bless you, me little Johneen, me little son; sure 'tis yourself has the decent, kind heart to be taking pity upon the old. Arrah now! You're alone and lonely this evening, I notice, for your friend is gone from you. It bees lonely when one loses one's comrade. Ah, 'tis many a year and more since I lost me comrade through the valley of life. Since Marks Prendergast, the good husband of me heart and the father of me children, was lost on me. Sure he was murdered on me one St. Patrick's Day fair in Garradrimna. He was ripped open with a knife and left there upon the street in his blood for me to see.... That's the way, that's the way, me sweet gosoon; some die clean and quiet, and some go away in their blood like the way they came."

Had she devoted much time and skill to it she could not have produced a more dire effect upon John than by this accidental turn of her talk.... The scene by the lakeside swam clearly into his eyes again.

"I suppose *your* good comrade is gone away?"

"Whom, what?"

"Ulick Shannon, to be sure. I suppose he's after slipping away be this time anyway."

"Aye, he's gone away."

"That was what you might call the nice lad. And it was no wonder at all that you were so much attached to one another. Never a bit of wonder at all.... Sure you were like brothers."

John was so solicitous in maintaining his silence that he did not notice the old woman's terrible sententiousness.... He went on pulling green sticks from the hedge and placing them very carefully by the side of those she had already gathered.

"Just like brothers. That's what ye were, just like brothers. He, he, he!"

Although he did not detect the note of laughter in it that was hollow and a mockery, he was nevertheless appalled by what should appear as a commendation of him who was gone.... He felt himself shaking even as the leaves in the hedgerows were being shaken by the light wind of evening.

"Like brothers, *avic machree.*"

Even still he did not reply.

"Like brothers, I say, and that's the whole story. For ye were brothers. At least you were of the one blood, because ye had the same woman for the mother of ye both."

Certainly she was raving, but her words were having an unusual effect upon him. He was keeping closer to the hedge as if trying to hide his face.

"To-night, me fine gosoon, I'm going to do a terrible thing. I'm going to tell you who your mother is, and then you'll know a quare story. You'll know that Ulick Shannon, good luck to him wherever he's gone, was nothing less than your own brother.... It is she that is after forcing me on to it be her penurious and miserly ways. I didn't want to tell ye, John! I say, I didn't want to tell ye!"

Her old, cracked voice trailed away into a high screech. John Brennan was like a man stunned by a blow as he waited for her to speak the rest of the story.

"Ulick Shannon's father, Henry Shannon, was the one your mother loved. She never cared for your father, nor he for her. So you might say you are no love child. But there was a love child in it to be sure, and that child was Ulick Shannon. Your mother was his mother. He was born out of wedlock surely, but he happened handy, and was put in the place of Grace Gogarty's child that died and it a weeshy, young thing.... It was your grandmother that sold him, God forgive her, if you want to know, for I was watching the deed being done.... Your mother always thought the bastard was murdered in the house and buried in the garden. I used to be forever tormenting her by making her think that only it was me could tell. There was no one knew it for certain in the whole world, only me and them that were dead and gone. So your mother could not have found out from any one but me, and she might never have found out only for the way she used to be refusing me of me little dues.... But I can tell you that she found out this evening how she was the mother of Ulick Shannon, and that you, the beloved son she cherished in her heart and put on in all her pride to be a priest of God, was a near blood relation of the boy she was never done but running down. The boy that she, above all others, with her prate and gab made a drunkard of in the first place, and then rushed on, be always talking of the like about him, to do great harm to this girl. But sure it was myself that could not blame him at all, for it was in him both ways, the poor, unfortunate gosoon!"

There was no reason to doubt the old shuiler's story, with such passionate vehemence did it fall from her. And its coherence was very convincing. It struck him as a greater blow which almost obliterated his understanding. In the first moment he could stand apart from it and look even blindly it appeared as the swift descent of Divine vengeance upon him for what he had just done.... He moved away, his mind a bursting tumult, and without a sight in his eyes.... The mocking laughter of Marse Prendergast rang in his ears. Now why was she laughing at him when it was his mother who was her enemy?

He was walking, but the action was almost unnoticed by him. He was moving aimlessly within the dark, encircling shadow of his doom.... Yet he saw that he was not far distant from Garradrimna.... The last time he had been there at the period of the day he had been in company with Ulick Shannon. It was what had sprung out of those comings together that was now responsible for this red ending.... He remembered also how the port wine had lifted him out of himself and helped him to see Rebecca Kerr.... The windows were squinting through the gloom as he went the road.

There was stronger drink in Garradrimna and pubs. of greater intensity than McDermott's. There was "The World's End," for instance, that tavern so fantastically named by the Hon. Reginald Moore in memory of an inn of the same name that had struck his fancy in England.... The title now seemed particularly appropriate.

It was towards this place his feet were moving. In another spell of thought which surprised him by the precaution it exhibited, he remembered that his father would not be there; for, although it had been Ned Brennan's famous haunt aforetime, he had been long ago forbidden its doors. It was in this, one of the seven places of degradation in Garradrimna, he was now due to appear.

He went very timidly up to the back-door, which opened upon a little, secluded passage. He ordered a glass of whiskey from the greasy barmaid who came to attend him.... He felt for the money so carefully wrapped in tissue-paper in his waistcoat pocket. It was a bright gold sovereign that his mother had given him on the first day of his course at Ballinamult College to keep against any time he might be called upon to show off the fact that he was a gentleman. As he unfolded it now, from the careful covering in which she had wrapped it, it seemed to put on a tragic significance.... He was fearfully anxious to be in the condition that had brought him his vision on the night he had slept by the lake.

He drank the whiskey at one gulp, and it seemed a long time until the barmaid returned with the change. Sovereigns were marvels of rare appearance at "The World's End." He thanked her and called for another, paying her as she went. She was remarkably mannerly, for, in the narrow gloom of the place, she took him to be some rich stranger. She had seen the color of his money and liked it well.

The whiskey seemed to possess magical powers. It rapidly restored him to a mood wherein the distress that was his might soon appear a small thing. Yet he grew restless with the urgency that was upon him and glanced around in search of a distraction for his galloping brain.... He bent down and peered through the little aperture which opened upon the public bar of "The World's End." In there he saw a man in a heated atmosphere and enveloped by dense clouds of tobacco-smoke. They were those who had come in the roads to forget their sweat and labor in the black joy of porter. Theirs was a part of the tragedy of the fields, but it was a meaner tragedy. Yet were they suddenly akin to him.... Through the lugubrious expression on their dark faces a sudden light was shining. It was the light as if of some ecstasy. A desire fell upon him to enter into their dream, whatever it might be.... In the wild whirl that the whiskey had whipped up in his brain there now came a sudden lull. It was a lull after a great crescendo, as in Beethoven's music.... He was hearing, with extraordinary clearness, what they were saying. They were speaking of the case of Ulick Shannon and Rebecca Kerr. These names were linked inseparably and were going hand in hand down all the byeways of their talk.... They were sure and certain that he had gone away. There was not a sign of him in Garradrimna this evening. That put the cap on his guilt surely. Wasn't she the grand whipster, and she supposed to be showing a good example and teaching religion to the childer? A nice one to have in the parish indeed! It was easy knowing from the beginning what she was and the fellow she struck up with—Henry Shannon's son. Wasn't that enough for you? Henry Shannon, who was the best blackguard of his time!... Just inside, and very near to John, a knot of men were discussing the more striking aspects of the powerful scandal.... They were recounting, with minute detail, the story of Nan Byrne.... Wasn't it the strangest thing now how she had managed more or less to live it down? But people would remember it all again in the light of this thing. What Ulick Shannon had done now would make people think of what his father had done, and then they must needs remember her.... And to think that no one ever knew rightly what had become of the child. Some there were who would tell you that her sister, Bridget Mulvey, and her mother, Abigail Byrne, buried it in the garden, and there were those who would tell you that it was living somewhere at the present time.... Her son John was not a bad sort, but wasn't it the greatest crime for her to put him on to be a priest after what had happened to her, and surely no good could come of it?... And why wouldn't Ned Brennan know of it, and wasn't it that and nothing else that had made him the ruined wreck of a man he was? Sure he'd never done a day's good since the night Larry Cully had lashed out the whole story for his benefit. And wasn't it quite possible that some one would be bad enough to tell John himself some time, or the ecclesiastical authorities? What about the mee-aw that had happened to him in the grand college in England that so much had been heard of? And there was sure to be something else happening before he was through the college at Ballinamult. A priest, how are ye?

The whiskey had gone to his head, but, as he listened, John Brennan felt himself grow more sober than he had ever before been.... So this was the supplement to the story he had heard a while ago. And now that he knew the whole story he began to tremble. Continually flashing across his mind were the words of the man who was dead and silent at the bottom of the lake— "You could never know a woman, you could never trust her; you could not even trust your own mother." This was a hard thing for any man at all to have said in his lifetime, and yet how full of grim, sad truth did it now appear?... The kind forgetfulness of his choking bitterness that he had so passionately longed for would not come to him.... The dregs of his heart were beginning to turn again towards thoughts of magnanimity as they had already done in the first, clear spell of thought after his deed. He had then gone to gather sticks for the old woman, a kind thing, as Jesus might have done in Nazareth.... The change of the sovereign was in his hand and his impulse was strong upon him. He could not resist. It seemed as if a strong magnet was pulling a light piece of steel.... He had walked into the public bar of "The World's End." Around him was a sea of faces, laughing, sneering, drinking, sweating, swearing, spitting. He was calling for a drink for himself and a round for the shop.... Now the sea of faces was becoming as one face. And there was a look upon it which seemed made up of incredulity and contempt.... This was replaced by a different look when the pints were in their hands.... They were saying: "Good health, Mr. Brennan!" with a sneer in their tones and a smile of flattery upon those lips which had just now been vomiting out the slime of their minds.

There was another and yet another round. As long as he could remain on his feet he remained standing drinks to them. There was a longing upon him to be doing this thing. And beyond it was the guiding desire to be rid of every penny of the sovereign his mother had given him to help him appear as a gentleman if he met company.... Now it seemed to soil him, coming as it did from her. Curious that feeling after all she had done for him, and she his mother. But it would not leave him.

The drink he had bought was fast trickling down the many throats that were burning to receive it. The rumor of his prodigality was spreading abroad through Garradrimna, and men had gone into the highways and the byeways to call their friends to the banquet. Two tramps on their way to the Workhouse had heard of it and were already deep in their pints. Upon John's right hand, arrived as if by magic, stood Shamesy Golliher, and upon his left the famous figure of Padna Padna, who was looking up into his face with admiration and brightness striving hard to replace the stare of vacancy in the dimming eyes. As he drank feverishly, fearful of losing any, Shamesy Golliher continuously ejaculated: "Me sweet fellow, John! Me sweet fellow!" And Padna Padna kept speaking to himself of the grand thing it was that there was one decent fellow left in the world, even if he was only Nan Byrne's son. Around John Brennan was a hum of flattery essentially in the same vein.... And it seemed to him that, in his own mind, he had soared far beyond them.... Outwardly he was drunk, but inwardly he knew himself to be very near that rapture which would bring thoughts of Rebecca as he staggered home alone along the dark road.

The companions of his Bacchic night had begun to drift away from him. Ten o'clock was on the point of striking, and he was in such a condition that he might be upon their hands at any moment. They did not want Walter Clinton, the proprietor of "The World's End," to be giving any of them the job of taking him home. The hour struck and the remnant went charging through the doorways like sheep through a gap. Shamesy Golliher limped out, leading Padna Padna by the hand, as if the ancient man had suddenly become metamorphosed into his second childishness.... "The bloody-looking idiot!" they were all sniggering to one another. "Wasn't it a hell of a pity that Ned Brennan, his father, and he always bowseying for drink in McDermott's and Brannagan's, wasn't in 'The World's End' to-night?"

John was alone amidst the dregs of the feast. Where the spilt drink was shining on the counter there was such a sight of glasses as he had never before seen. There were empty glasses and glasses still standing with half their drink in them, and glasses in which the porter had not been touched so drunk had everybody been.

Walter Clinton came in indignantly and said that it was a shame for him to be in such a state, and to go home out of that at once before the peelers got a hold of him.... And he went out with difficulty and down the old road of the elms towards his mother's house in the valley. He could hear the hurrying, heavy feet of those he had entertained so lavishly far down before him on the road.... For the moment he was happy. Before his burning eyes was the form of Rebecca Kerr. Her face had a look of quiet loveliness. He thought it was like the faces of the Madonnas in Father O'Keeffe's parlor.... "Rebecca! Rebecca!" he called to her ever in the agony of his love. "Thy hands, dear Rebecca!" ... She was not soiled now by any earthly sin, for he had purified her through the miracle of blood. And she was clean like the night wind.

He was a pitiable sight as he went staggering on, crying out this ruined girl's name to the night silence of the lonely places.... At last he fell somewhere in the soft, dewy grass. For a long while he remained here—until he began to realize that his vision was passing with the decline within him of the flame by which it had been created. The winds upon his face and hair were cold, and it seemed that he was lying in a damp place. His eyes sprang open.... He was lying by the lakeside and at the place where he had murdered Ulick Shannon.

He jumped up of a sudden, for his fear had come back to him. With his mouth wide open and a clammy sweat upon his brow, he started to run across what seemed a never-ending grassy space.... He broke madly through fences of thorn and barbed wire, which tore his clothes and his hands. He stumbled across fields of tillage.... At last, with every limb shivering, he came near his mother's door.... Presently he grew coldly conscious.... He could hear his father muttering drunkenly within. He came nearer, striving hard to steady himself and walk erect. He quickened his step to further maintain his pretense of sobriety. His foot tripped against something, and he lurched forward. He was caught in his mother's arms, for, at the sound of his approach, she had opened the door in resigned and mournful expectation.

"O Jesus!" she said.

There were two of them now.

THE END

Milton Keynes UK
Ingram Content Group UK Ltd.
UKHW030740071024
449371UK00006B/683

9 789362 091314